# PRESCRIPTION FOR
# EXTREME HEALTH

Nationally renowned author, speaker, radio, and TV personality
shares his revolutionary take on getting well and staying well

# DR. JOE ESPOSITO

BONUS
SECTION!
Dr. Joe's Nutrition
Prescription for
Extreme Athletes

*Health Plus Publishing*
MARIETTA, GEORGIA

For ordering information, contact Health Plus Publishing, 950
Cobb Pkwy. S., #190, Marietta, GA 30060, (770)-427-7387,
www.DrJoeEsposito.com.

*Project Manager:* Marla Markman
www.marlamarkman.com

*Cover and Interior Design:* GKS Creative
www.gkscreative.com

978-0-9978730-0-9 (Softcover)
978-0-9978730-2-3 (eReaders)

Printed in the United States of America

FIRST EDITION
20 19 18 17 16 / 10 9 8 7 6 5 4 3 2 1

*This book is dedicated with much love to my parents, Rose Marie and Joe Esposito, the greatest parents ever.*

# Table of Contents

**BONUS
SECTION!**

# Introduction

# Not Your Average Joe

A patient once said to me: "You know, Dr. Joe, you're not your Average Joe."

Whenever I speak, I generally get the same reaction from my audiences. I usually hear people gasping in disbelief as they react to what I'm saying. And I can see their eyes getting as large as quarters because they are so shocked by the extreme health secrets that I share with them.

That's why I named this book *Dr. Joe's Secrets of Extreme Health*.

Most people who come to hear me speak have more than an average interest in their health. They have started to push the envelope a bit in their quest for better health, but they don't know who or what to believe.

I don't know where YOU are in that process, but I expect that you, too, will be shocked by the extreme secrets I share. Even though a lot of what I share is common sense, most Americans have never really considered how some of the things they do on a daily basis contribute to their lack of robust health.

I'm here to guide you through this "extreme shocking process." You're going to be amazed at the information you learn from this book. Some of it, quite frankly, will gross you out; some of it will produce what I call *aha moments*, and some will cause something to "click" in your brain regarding things that have been going on in your body for years.

You'll find that I repeat several messages over and over in this book. Science has shown us that we must hear information 11 times for our brains to remember and "groove" data into our neural pathways so that it can be accessed easily. That's why you will find important information repeated in different ways throughout this book.

Just think about how many times you see or hear radio or TV commercials. You begin to memorize them without even trying! By repeating certain important messages throughout the book, I'm helping you to learn more—faster!

But before we begin this shocking journey of extreme secrets together, I'd like to share how I got here.

I was born in New Jersey and lived in Hoboken for the first eight years of my life. My dad, who never graduated from high school, came from a family of 10 children and became a sign hanger as an adult. Like all his brothers and sisters, my dad worked hard and turned his paychecks over to the family, because that's the way it was back then.

About four months before I was born, something happened to my dad that changed all of our lives forever. He and one of his co-workers, Charlie, had finished hanging a sign and were getting ready to break for lunch. Back then, fancy hydraulics were not used for everyday jobs, so my dad used a crank ladder. (For you young whippersnappers who don't know what a crank ladder is, it is a ladder that lengthens or shortens by means of a hand-crank. That is manual labor in the truest sense.)

As my dad and Charlie were breaking for lunch, the ladder got stuck. Now, my dad was a bit of an adventurer, so he began to climb up the ladder, hoping his weight would force the ladder to come down and fix their problem. But, instead of sliding back into normal position, the ladder fell backward—into traffic on a busy street—with my father underneath! He fell about three stories—30 feet—and landed on his butt, and then fell backward, striking his head.

Luckily, a nearby traffic light was red and no cars were coming. However, once he landed in the street, he realized he couldn't hear. "Charlie, Charlie. I can't hear anything," my dad shouted frantically. Then he passed out.

I've heard this story many times, but my father didn't actually remember any of this. Isn't it amazing how the brain sometimes protects us from painful memories? At the hospital, doctors discovered my dad had fractured his back and his skull. He slipped in and out of a coma, and the fall caused him to go deaf instantly.

My mother, who was five months pregnant with me, had to take care of my toddler sister and my dad at the same time. She had no skills to support the family financially. The entire family was frantic, trying to figure out how we were going to survive without my father to care for us.

My father was still in the hospital, mummified in a body cast, when I was born in a different hospital.

In those days, if you were deaf, you couldn't get a job. There were no "hire the handicapped" programs, OSHA laws, or anything like that. We only received a tiny bit of support from the government and some workman's compensation funds. So, we grew up, as they say, "rich in love."

The most interesting part was that I never knew we were poor because all of my friends and their families were pretty much in the same boat. Nobody ever told us we were poor!

I grew up with a great dad. When everyone else's fathers had to leave and go to work, my dad got to stay home with me. He was always there to teach me a lot of life lessons: how to fix a bicycle, how to change a flat tire, how to install a window, how to unclog a drain. Since we didn't have a lot of money, my dad had to do these things himself, and since he had a bad back and was deaf, I became his "Italian muscle."

"Joey, go get this. Joey, go get that." All day long, I'd run back and forth, fetching and "toting" stuff for him. From as far back as I can remember, Dad would complain about his back hurting. In my mind, I can still hear him saying, "Joey, rub my back. Joey, rub my back."

That was the way I bonded with my dad. I'd do my best with my little boy hands, and he'd tell me how great it felt. Instant positive reinforcement, as the brainiacs call it. I never forgot how great it made me feel to make him feel better. I made up my mind to be a neurosurgeon. I was going to be the superhero who would operate on Dad to fix his back and restore his hearing. I was going to make him all better. Since the doctors said he had nerve deafness, I should be able to fix it when I became a neurosurgeon, right?

As I began my pre-med undergraduate work, I began to learn how the body worked. As I continued to research nerves and how they affect and work in the body, my grandmother suggested that I go to a chiropractor's office. "Why don't you go see my chiropractor? He does something with nerves."

So one day I walked into a chiropractor's office looking young and naïve, and began to pick the doctor's brain. He couldn't have been nicer. He began to go through all of his charts, diagrams, and drawings with me, explaining how everything in the body works and how chiropractic care can assist in the process of repairing and maintaining nerve function. I was fascinated and said to myself, "This makes sense."

I always love it when people listen to my radio and TV shows or attend one of my lectures and say, "Dr. Joe, what you say really makes sense." That's when I know I've done a good job.

I remember going home and telling my mom, "I think I want to be a chiropractor." Her response? (Parents, pay attention here.) "I don't care if you want to be a garbage man, as long as you're the best garbage man you can possibly be." You can't beat that for motherly love, can you?

While I was in undergraduate school, one of my professors was the lead author of the best-selling anatomy and physiology books in the world. He said to me, "Joe, you're the smartest male student I've ever had in my career. What do you want to do with your life?" I told him I wanted to be a chiropractor. He said, "With your grades and my recommendation, you can get into any medical school you want. Are you sure that's what you want?"

I thought about it long and hard. I'm not against surgery. I'm not against drugs. But I am against the *unnecessary* use of drugs and surgery. I was fascinated by chiropractic care because it addresses the root cause of the problems, not just the symptoms.

I love what I do. People love to get adjusted. They feel better immediately. It's that instant positive reinforcement for me. They feel better. I feel better. It takes me back to the days when my dad used to ask me to rub his back. My father was the first person I ever adjusted as a chiropractor. That moment will never leave my memory or my heart.

You may be curious to know what happened to my dad. Through chiropractic care, he was able to regain much of his energy and vitality. And yes, until the end of his life, I kept rubbing his back! Because his bones had never set right after the accident, my father experienced excruciating pain for many years—until I became a chiropractor and started adjusting him. Although my father never regained his hearing, with chiropractic adjustments and the knowledge that I passed on to him, he was able to live a full life well into his 70s, during which time he enjoyed complete mobility, and he felt better and had less pain.

This is one reason I am so sensitive to people who are living lives full of pain. I understand how that kind of pain affects the entire family. When a family member is in excruciating pain, everyone in the family suffers. I'm grateful that I gained the knowledge to help reduce or even alleviate such pain and suffering in my patients.

Though not as catastrophic as my father's ordeal, I have had my own issues. Don't break out the tissues just yet. It's not what you think.

As a child, I suffered from sinus problems, hives, allergies to just about everything, and I was overweight. I think I took every drug known to man in an attempt to cure my health problems, yet—at best—they stayed the same. And on bad days, I could hardly breathe. I am sure I had what is now known as attention deficit disorder, and was in constant trouble in school and at home. My fingers were constantly twitching; my sleep patterns were a mess; and my lips and eyes would swell up to the point that it was comical. To everyone except me, that is.

One day, while in college, I remember waking up and not feeling bad. I actually felt good. I didn't know why. Then, I remembered that one of my instructors had said that what you eat can have an effect on how you feel.

So I decided to write down everything I had eaten and done for the previous few days. I realized I had consumed a very good diet including lots of fruits, vegetables, nuts, and seeds. I had avoided alcohol, meat, sugar, dairy, coffee, soda, and artificial sweeteners. I had gotten lots of rest and a good amount of exercise. As an experiment, I put a few of my "usual suspect" poisons—alcohol, meat, sugar, dairy, coffee, soda, and artificial sweeteners—back into my diet. Sure enough, I began to feel worse again.

For me, this was the beginning of a crusade that will last the rest of my life. I made a commitment to learn and teach others how to prevent disease and treat the causes of illnesses, not just try to cover up the symptoms. That's why, for many years, as an adjunct to my chiropractic practice, I have been lecturing on the subject of nutrition.

I've been where many of you are now, and I understand what you are going through. You need to change your perspective on your life. If you do, you will find it is not difficult to change your lifestyle; it is just a different way of living. You have to eat anyway so why not eat healthy food?

This book is designed to teach you how to make simple changes in your life that can make the difference between health and disease, and even life and death. Allow me to teach you why it's wise to convert to a primarily plant-based diet. I promise that once you try it, you'll be mad at yourself that you didn't do this sooner.

This lifestyle is easy, healthy, and a great way to:

- Lose weight without dieting
- Have fun while learning interesting new information
- Be kind to the environment
- Save money on food
- Maintain a cleaner kitchen
- Add many quality years to your life

# Dr. Joe's Credentials

If you're into credentials and want to know mine, here goes:

- Magna Cum Laude Degree in Chiropractic from Life University in Marietta, Georgia;
- Diplomate in orthopedics from the American Board of Chiropractic Orthopedics;
- Diplomate in pain management from the American Academy of Pain Management in Modesto, California;
- Diplomate from the College of Clinical Nutrition and the Chiropractic Board of Clinical Nutrition;
- Bachelor's of science in clinical nutrition from Life University in Marietta, Georgia;
- Licensed dietician (retired); and
- Honorary Brother Award from the Chi-Rho Professional Fraternity.

It's no accident that I chose this area of study. It is my firm belief that, along with eating a proper diet, you must have a normally functioning nervous system and digestive system. These are the most crucial determinants of long-term health, and in my speeches and with my patients, I discuss how the standard American diet (SAD) frankly does a number on our health.

It is also no accident that this book came into your life, into your path, and in front of you at this particular time. I hope you read it with a positive mind-set and a determination to make your life a better place to live! You *are* going to be shocked by some of the secrets you will read in this book.

But even more shocking is this secret wisdom that most people never discover: *If you do not take time to be healthy, you will have to take time to be sick.*

I've been a practicing nutritionist and chiropractor for decades now. Most people who come into my office are—quite frankly—in pretty bad shape. Shockingly, they have no idea how they got that way. They don't understand why even though they go to the doctor and take their meds, they're not getting any better.

Most folks will agree that it's a good idea to take care of their bodies in order to attain and maintain good health. The problem is most people don't know *what to do*, or if they do know, they don't have the willpower or self-discipline to make the changes. And they are bombarded with data (both correct and incorrect) regarding various types of diets, treatments, and diagnoses. It's not like there is a lack of knowledge or information on the subject. Everywhere you turn, there's a new diet book, new research about the effects of certain foods, or a new guaranteed-to-get-results exercise program.

You should have everything you may, or may not, want to know about taking care of your body, right? The problem is, people no longer know what or who to believe regarding their health. My patients generally have an idea that there *should* be a better way, but they just don't know how to get there.

# "Be careful about reading health books. You may die of a misprint."
## —Mark Twain

Then, there are the people who seem to know "the secret." They never seem to age, get tired, wrinkled, or sick. Have you ever met one of these extremely healthy people? You probably get tired just watching them work endless hours, spend time with their families, work out, and achieve amazing life results. Do you just want to smack them because they seem to have the secret of life and you don't? Or do you sincerely and deeply desire to know the secrets that they hold? How is it that some people have the "magic formula" and some don't? It doesn't seem fair.

Believe it or not, most of the "magic formula" involves having the correct information. The ones without this information feel like they're on the outside looking through the window at people who have amazingly healthy lives, even into their 80s, 90s, and beyond.

If there were a simple, easy-to-understand, step-by-step method of accessing this information and improving your life, would you do it? I have posed this question to several hundred people, and most of them resoundingly said they would change their lives for the better if they just knew how.

That's why I then surveyed extremely healthy people to find out how they can be healthy and still live a normal life. What I discovered changed my life and the lives of many of my patients forever. From that research, I compiled this book. The following chapters provide a simple outline of what these healthy people do, what they know, and how they live their lives. In addition, I've given you some of my "hidden" knowledge, which most people have never taken the time to learn and the media have never taken the time to explain.

Now I'm a realist, folks, and I realize some of you won't do *everything* that I say in this book. That's okay. This is "brown belt" nutrition. When you're ready to go "black belt," we'll need to sit and talk.

But do *something*. When you make one little change, you'll say, "Gee, that wasn't so hard." And then you'll make another little change. And another little change.

When you do, start looking for some subtle changes in your life and health. You might notice you sleep better, go to the bathroom better, have a better love life, have more strength and energy. Overall, you feel better, and your life just starts getting better.

This is your chance to discover the SECRETS TO EXTREME HEALTH. Don't let it pass you by!

# "You needn't be well to be wealthy, but you've got to be whole to be holy."

## From one of Dr. Joe's favorite songs,

## "Hallowed Be Thy Name" by Emerson, Lake, & Palmer,

## from the album Works, Volume 1

*(If you don't know this band, go ask your dad!)*

CHAPTER 1

# Stop Poisoning Yourself!

**E**xtremely healthy people understand that Poison was an '80s rock band (ask your dad) who made music you should listen to—not what you should be taking into your body. So, your first step to maximizing your health is to stop poisoning yourself.

You're probably thinking, "Now, come on, Dr. Joe, I'm not doing anything crazy like putting poisons in my body. What do you mean?"

I mean that you have to stop putting the things in your body that short-circuit your energy, vitality, and your ability to fight off disease, illness, and aging.

## Dr. Joe's "No Poison" Plan

Imagine that you knew your friend had a secret formula that could help you get well and stay well. Would you want to know the formula? Would it be worth $1,000? $10,000? $100,000?

In this book, you will find the not-so-secret formula that has worked for me, my family, my friends, and tens of thousands of my followers, patients, and listeners. I will reveal some shocking health secrets that you must know and the steps you must take to obtain and maintain great health. Notice I didn't just say good health—I said GREAT health. Good health may be good enough for some people, but because you have this book in your hands, I already know you don't want to settle for good health.

These extreme health secrets will show you how to:

- Repair and maintain a normally functioning nervous system.
- Repair and maintain a normally functioning digestive system.
- Follow a good nutrition plan.

This book will show you the steps you need to take to achieve each of these pathways to great health. These days, there's so much information that people are completely overwhelmed and confused about who to trust. My goal in writing this book is to teach you about how your body works so that you can use that knowledge as a tool to have an amazing life. You don't want just good health, right? You want amazing health!

I wish I had a dollar for every patient who has said to me, "Dr. Joe, if I'd only known these secrets sooner, I could have saved myself years of pain and suffering." If I had those dollars, I'd be writing this book from my own private island, instead of from beautiful Marietta, Georgia (home of the Big Chicken. Google it for grins.)

It seems there are more advertisements every day for a new drug to help with ailments, from cancer to menstrual cramps. I want to start by saying I am *not* against the use of prescription drugs, but I am against drug *misuse* and *abuse*.

Our society has been taught that if something is wrong with our health, we need to take a pill to make ourselves better. I think there is a better way to make us feel great: by building up and maintaining the immune system so we are less likely to get sick. Let's get educated and create habits that help prevent us from getting sick in the first place.

And in many cases, getting sick may not be such a bad thing. Getting sick is a sign that our immune system has been overloaded and is no longer able to deal with a particular problem in a *subclinical* manner. What does that mean? In this case, "subclinical" means the body is working on a problem internally, but we experience no obvious symptoms indicating that there is a problem until the immune system gets overloaded and we get sick.

When that happens, it's much wiser to determine why our body has been unable to deal with the problem subclinically—then we can correct the cause, not just treat the symptoms. For some people, this is a shocking approach. For me, it is the logical, smart, scientific, and natural secret to extreme, great health.

The opportunity for an extremely healthy life awaits you, and you may need to make only a few small lifestyle changes to get there. The following chapters will provide more details about those changes, but let's end this chapter where we began: talking about poison.

These harmful foods will poison your body and cause the most damage to the immune system. I call them the "Seven Deadly Sins of Nutrition":

1. Alcohol
2. Meat
3. Dairy
4. Sugar
5. Coffee
6. Soda
7. Artificial sweeteners

Many of you just cried out, "That's my whole diet"!

I'll explain each of the seven deadly sins in detail in Chapter 5. But first you need to know more about a healthy digestive system, so that's where we will start in Chapter 2.

# "'Tis healthy to be sick sometimes."
# —Henry David Thoreau

# Dr. Joe's #1 Secret of Extreme Health:

## The Digestive System

The father of medicine, Hippocrates, reportedly said, "All disease begins in the gut."

If that's true, do you find it as unbelievable as I do that medical schools traditionally have spent nearly zero time on nutrition? Thankfully, this is turning around and nutrition studies are gaining traction, but academia's focus on drugs and surgery have made them the foundation of Western medicine for centuries. The cornerstone of Eastern medicine? Good digestion. This chapter explains the physical and mechanical aspects of how your digestive system works. What you should eat will be discussed further in later chapters.

The basic needs of your "gut" may sound complicated, confusing, and just a touch embarrassing. But I am not referring to the beer belly you have so lovingly created and tended for so many years. I am referring to the internal workings of your digestive system.

# A SAD State of Affairs

Having been in practice for several decades, I have found that a majority of patients experience some type of digestive problem, but few are willing to talk about it. In fact, I would say 85 percent of my patients tell me they have digestive problems and 15 percent lie! In my experience, everyone has some kind of digestive problem.

A good percentage of all emergency room visits are related to the digestive system, which surprised even me, as I primarily think of the ER as a place for trauma patients. But when you think about it, you don't have to have a steering wheel rupture your intestines to cause trauma to your digestive system.

I call the standard American diet "SAD" for short. (Isn't that ironic?) This diet perpetrates intestinal trauma on an incremental and exponential basis every day.

It seems that in our society, we can talk about cancer, heart disease, diabetes, osteoporosis, and even erectile dysfunction and not feel embarrassment. However, digestive problems—one of our most common ailments—are apparently a taboo subject to discuss out loud.

Digestive problems are not only uncomfortable—and sometimes embarrassing—they also have a direct link to your overall physical and mental health. We spend billions of dollars each year attempting to cover up the symptoms of digestive problems, but very few doctors tell their patients how to actually correct the problems—or better yet—how to avoid the problems. That's why digestive disorders can snowball from mild discomfort all the way to cancer.

# The Mechanics of Digestion

Digestion starts when you think about food. For example, try thinking about a big, juicy lemon. In your mind, take that lemon and slice it into quarters. Now take that lemon quarter, put it in your mouth, and start sucking on it.

What happened while you were thinking about sucking on that lemon? You started salivating, didn't you? So digestion actually starts when you think about your food. Cool, huh? Saliva's main job is to break down carbohydrates. That's why it's important to actually enjoy your food—so that you can produce enough saliva to process it.

Then you swallow your food, and it goes into your stomach. Your stomach's main job is to digest proteins in your food and break them down into amino acids. The food is then passed into your small intestines where it comes into contact with digestive enzymes produced in your pancreas. There are enzymes to help break down the proteins further, along with enzymes to help digest carbohydrates and fats.

There are actually three primary types of digestive enzymes—protease, amylase, and lipase. Their jobs are to break down the proteins, carbohydrates, and fats. This is why it is so important to take care of your pancreas—and also why pancreatic cancer is so deadly. It robs the body of the ability to digest food and break these proteins, carbohydrates, and fats into amino acids. If you don't have the ability to do this, you can die. Most people think that the pancreas' main job is just to produce insulin, but it is much more than that.

Your gallbladder stores bile, which digests fats. When you eat what I call a "big, fatty meal," your gallbladder squirts bile into this fat and dissolves it. Have you ever squirted liquid dishwashing detergent into a greasy pan and watched how the detergent seems to just dissolve the grease? That's what your gallbladder does—it dissolves the fats so you can absorb them.

## Absorbing Your Fats

If you've had your gallbladder removed, it's very important that you are careful about what types of fats you eat because you don't have this reserve of "dish detergent" to break the fats down properly. It's vital that you stay away from "difficult to digest" fats such as hydrogenated oils, animal fats, trans fats, even vegetable oils. Vegetable oils such as peanut, corn, and cottonseed are very high in omega-6 fatty acids and can cause a tremendous amount of inflammation; if not digested properly, they can cause some major problems.

"Good" fats would be extra-virgin organic coconut oil, extra-virgin olive oil, macadamia nut oil, avocado oil, and oils from other nuts and seeds. The "bad" fats are the ones that are processed chemically or mechanically altered.

Then your small intestine absorbs the nutrients and passes what's left into the large intestine. Your large intestine absorbs water then packs what's left of your lunch into fecal matter, which is passed out of the body.

So your digestive system is a very complex mechanism with very complex responsibilities. Imagine you're eating a hamburger. Your body needs to be able to digest the burger, break it down, and reassemble it as body parts, such as toenails, hair, skin, lungs, and so forth.

We often take our digestive system for granted. We just shove stuff in our bodies and assume it's going to work. Eventually, stuff will cause damage, and you will have to pay the piper.

# The Enzymes of Digestion

So, back to digestive enzymes. Protease breaks down proteins into something called amino acids, so we can absorb them. Once they're absorbed, they get "reassembled" into different things, and enzymes play a key role in that process as well.

While some enzymes break down food, others act kind of like matchmakers. The matchmaker enzymes say, "Hey you, you molecule over there, you come meet this molecule over here. You guys go make some eye tissue; you guys over there, go make a toenail." Some of the molecules become liver; some become skin. Our digestive system has to break down proteins and reassemble them so they can rebuild organs.

Amylase is the stuff in your saliva that helps break down the sugars in carbohydrates into small components that can be utilized everywhere else in the body. Lipase breaks down fats. Enzymes will also attack invaders. You have an infection? Enzymes can help deal with that infection.

Every single function of your body happens because of enzymes. When you're young, you have lots of enzymes in your body, but you don't produce as many enzymes when you get older, and cooked and processed foods require more enzymes to break them down. That's why it's so important to eat raw foods: they help replace the enzymes that you're using up.

Remember being a teenager? You could drink a six-pack, eat a large pepperoni pizza, sleep for two hours, wake up the next day and do it all over again? Remember those days?

Can't do that anymore, can you? One reason you can't is because you're not able to digest your food like you used to. Do you know what little kids eat? French fries and sugary cereal, and, BAM, they grow! There are almost no nutrients in French fries, yet the kids keep getting taller, stronger, and smarter (well, we hope) every day. Where's the nutrition coming from?

Part of the explanation is that a child or young adult's digestive enzymes are so strong, they can extract whatever nutrients are in the foods they're eating. As you get older, you can't do it anymore.

### The Vinegar Experiment

Humor me. Try an experiment. This might work for some of you.

Drink some raw, organic apple cider vinegar. It will promote good digestion because it's rich in enzymes and potassium. It also helps to support a healthy immune system by keeping the pH level in an alkaline state.

Did you know that in 400 BC, Hippocrates, the Father of Medicine, used apple cider vinegar as a cleansing and healing agent? You remember him. He's the guy who said that all health is a factor in digestion.

Studies have shown that raw, organic apple cider vinegar is effective in helping control blood glucose and insulin levels by reducing the glycemic index of foods. Research also supports the use of it for weight loss and for diabetes.

This is how I use apple cider vinegar. I have 24 ounces of water sitting on my nightstand next to my bed; before I go to bed, I put two tablespoons of raw organic apple cider vinegar in the water. The next morning, I drink it—before I do anything else. Doesn't sound too hard, does it?

Why in the cat hair (as they strangely say in the South, where I transplanted to from my native New Jersey) would I pull this seemingly crazy stunt?

I do it, and I'm encouraging you to do it, dear reader, because, statistically speaking, almost everyone is clinically dehydrated, and you need water for a normally functioning digestive system. There are many reasons that vinegar helps create a healthy digestive system, including the fact that it's loaded with enzymes and beneficial bacteria and can help calm the digestive system.

So try my amazing alkaline digestive experiment! For some of you, it's going to do wonders! Just try it. I've always wanted my success strategies to be easy, simple, and doable, because if they're not, you won't do them. But if you try one and feel the benefits, you will be willing to try my other suggestions.

## Understanding pH Levels

Sometimes the body is very acidic, which causes the nerves to become more sensitive to pain. If you eat the standard American diet, chances are you are too acidic. If you are too acidic, it can adversely affect several bodily functions, including your nervous system, which controls everything.

Other types of vinegars stay acidic when they are ingested into in your body; however, raw organic apple cider vinegar becomes alkaline when you ingest it. That's one *aha moment* for you.

Apple cider vinegar is alkaline-forming because of its "ash" content, which means when it is digested, what is left over becomes ash. When you check for the pH of that ash and dissolve it in water, the content is alkaline. Whenever our body digests anything, it undergoes oxidation, and the end result is that you can determine whether the product was alkaline or acid.

Some other foods, such as celery, spinach, and figs, are also very alkalizing. Water is one of the most alkalizing things you can put into your body. Once your digestive system starts to calm down, then you're on the road to extreme health.

One foolproof way to determine whether your body is in an acidic state is to measure your body's pH levels. It's a fairly simple process to test your urine and saliva for pH levels. Take a strip of pH test paper, which you can find in any drug or health food store, and pass the paper through your urine stream first thing in the morning.

You'll see that different colors on the enclosed chart represent different pH levels. A urine pH level of 6.5 to 7.0 would be a great morning measurement.

To test your saliva, moisten the pH strip with your saliva as soon as you get out of bed in the morning. Do this before you brush your teeth or even think about eating. Ideally, your morning saliva pH should be 7.1 to 7.5.

If your body is too acidic, the urine pH levels will be below 6.5, and you need to understand what you're doing to cause those elevated levels. Diet, environmental toxins, stress, insufficient water, constipation, pinched nerves, and many other issues can cause an acidic state in your body.

## Hydration and the Body

The pancreas needs good water to produce the baking soda-like substance that neutralizes the acidic food coming from your stomach into your small intestine. And if you're dehydrated, you don't produce enough of this neutralizing substance, so the food stays in the stomach.

In these days of sports drinks, bottled water, and endless reminders to hydrate, why are we all dehydrated? It's really simple. Because we don't drink enough water.

Why not? Because when we are young a part of our brain controls hunger and another part of our brain controls thirst. But as we get older, the hunger center and thirst center of our brain grow together.

Another *aha moment*, isn't it? As the thirst center and hunger center grow together, we think we're hungry, but we're really *thirsty*. And so you eat something, and you're not thirsty anymore. But you didn't drink any water.

Okay, I'm going to share a secret way for you to stimulate the thirst center of your brain: drink more water.

If you drink more water, you actually "wake up" the area of your brain that will stimulate your thirst center. It's that simple. So if you start your day with water and raw organic apple cider vinegar, you are going to stimulate your digestive processes, which can help you meet your daily need for water. I recommend about six to eight glasses of water a day.

One way to tell if you are drinking enough water is to look at the color of your pee. It should be clear enough to read a newspaper through. (Don't try this—it will most likely get you in trouble for making a mess on the bathroom floor!) Your pee should also be odorless, and it should not have things floating in it. If it does have either of these, be sure to tell your doctor.

## What Kind of Water?

When it comes to water, my feeling is that the best water you can drink is freshly distilled water. Unfortunately, that's not very practical, because you have to get a distiller, and it takes a lot of work.

There are some arguments over distilled water. Some people like it. Some people don't. Some say they think it's great, but it takes all minerals out of the water. Good. I don't want to get minerals from my water. I want to get minerals from my fruits, vegetables, nuts, and seeds. That's where we should get minerals.

Most minerals in water come from rocks. It's called inorganic or nonliving sources of the minerals, and those are not as well absorbed as the organic minerals that come from fruits, vegetables, nuts, and seeds. Plant-based minerals are preferable because plants can take an inorganic mineral and convert it to an organic mineral.

Now remember that the word "organic" means from a living source. "Inorganic" (for the purposes of this conversation) means from rocks. So I want to get those inorganic minerals out of my system. End of argument.

People also ask me, "Doesn't distilled water leach minerals out of your system?" Yes, distilled water will flush some things out of your body, including a lot of waste products. As long as you're eating a good diet and you have a good digestive system and a healthy nervous system, this is no big deal.

If you're going to buy distilled water, make sure it's in a glass container. You can buy distilled water anywhere, but it's usually sold in a plastic container, which turns something good into something bad. The plastic container can leach toxic chemicals into the water.

Distilling your own water remains my first choice, but it is not very practical for most folks. Buying a distiller can be expensive; the process can take a long time, and there's a lot of wasted water. Using a distiller takes a lot of time to produce enough to drink and use on a daily basis, so it may not be the most cost-effective option.

The next best option, in my mind, is a reverse osmosis system, which is a pretty simple thing to acquire for your home. You can go to any do-it-yourself home store and get a reverse osmosis filter. It will cost you a few hundred dollars, but this equipment is well worth it, and it's usually easy to install. Just put it under your sink, and you're in business. You can drink the reverse osmosis water and wash your fruits and vegetables in it.

Personally, I have a filter at my house that's almost five feet tall, which filters every drop of water that comes into my house. I want to make sure I don't have chlorine, chemicals, and toxins on clothes I wash, and I don't want to sit in bathwater or take a shower with toxic chemicals that can be absorbed into my skin. One hot shower or bath can expose you to as many chemicals as you would get while drinking an eight-ounce glass of tap water. The heat opens up your pores, and your body absorbs the chemicals—and your skin is your largest organ. I don't want chlorine and fluoride gases released from my toilet. Every time you flush, these toxic gases are being sprayed into the air.

# Chemical Waste

A friend of mine had an unusual experience. Her husband was in the hospital for a long time. After she sat with him for three days, she went home to get some rest. When she urinated at home, she could smell the hospital. She had literally absorbed the cleaning chemicals into her body, although she had had no physical contact with them!

You may not be able to filter all your water the way I do right now or install special equipment. At a minimum, then, get a pitcher with a high-quality filter. Keep in mind that filtered or reverse osmosis purified water is going to be your best bet to put into your body.

Don't be fooled into thinking all you need is bottled water. Many times, the chemicals from the plastic bottle can leach into the water. In addition, if you read bottled water labels, they often identify the water as being from "a commercial or industrial source"—which could mean the original source is tap water. Just because water's in a bottle doesn't mean it's good. And just because the water has "springs" in its name doesn't mean it comes from an unspoiled spring somewhere. It may come out of a tap—just the same as the water in your house.

# Digestion and Mental Health Issues

People are constantly asking me what I know about clinical depression, bipolar disorder, and anxiety disorders, and how to deal with them without resorting to medications. What the general public does not know, understand, or seemingly care about is that many neurotransmitters, which play a large role in depression and other similar mental and emotional disorders, are produced in the gut.

As noted above, when you eat a protein, it goes into your stomach, and your stomach acids (hydrochloric acid and pepsin) break down the proteins into something called amino acids. Then the amino acids go into your small intestine where they are absorbed. The amino acid tryptophan combines with vitamin B6 in your body, creating a chemical called 5-HTP, which becomes serotonin. Some of that serotonin then becomes melatonin. Serotonin is one of the critical neurotransmitters affecting mood, sleep, and focus, and if you're not producing enough, your mood is going to be dramatically affected.

Up to 95 percent of the serotonin in your body is not utilized in your brain but is absorbed in your digestive system. So if you only have a little bit of serotonin because you're not absorbing the raw materials from your food, there is a battle for those raw materials because there's not enough to go around. That battle is going to affect the digestive system, which in turn affects your body's ability to absorb amino acids to produce serotonin. Not enough proteins broken down properly equals inability to sleep plus mood instability. You may not need more protein; you just need to better absorb the protein you're already consuming.

Tyrosine is an amino acid that becomes dopamine. Dopamine is the neurotransmitter that gives you pleasure, and pleasure gives a reason to live. We want to make sure the body is *absorbing* these nutrients so it has the raw materials to produce the neurotransmitters that help you live a happier life.

GABA is another important neurotransmitter, but with a different type of job: to suppress other neurotransmitters. In fact, GABA's main job, as with many of the nerves in your brain, is to suppress other nerves so that they keep you from having twitches and seizures. If you are not getting the proper amino acids, you are not producing the proper neurotransmitters.

So many of the psychological disorders I see in my patients do not begin "in the brain" as they think, but in the gut. So if we can fix the gut, the brain has a better chance to heal.

Years ago we used to think that once a brain cell was dead, it was dead forever. Well, it turns out we were wrong. Research now shows that the brain can regenerate certain cells, and many times it can rewire itself around damaged parts of the brain. It's called "neural plasticity," and that's what happens when a person starts to recover functions lost in a stroke.

In order for the brain to rewire itself, it is ultra-important that the digestive system be working correctly so you can absorb the nutrients you need to produce the neurotransmitters your brain needs to function properly. And remember, the nervous system controls everything, and we have to give the nervous system the proper nutrition, oxygen, and stimulation in order for it to work. That's why it's so important to focus on giving our gut the ability to produce more neurotransmitters.

I've never had a patient diagnosed with ADD/ADHD, bipolar disorder, anxiety disorder, or clinical depression who didn't have severe digestive problems. And when we work on the digestive problems, in most cases they improve—dramatically.

Is improving digestion the only thing my patients diagnosed with mood disorders need to do? Usually not. But this *must* be the first step.

The level of neurotransmitter production must increase in order to create more mood stability. Once you fix the gut, then the other stuff is easier to work with. The body must absorb the nutrients to produce the chemicals, specifically serotonin, so the brain can make the rest of the body work properly.

# Digestive Disorders:

# Why the Rumbly in the Tummy?

Now that we've covered the mechanics of digestion, let's talk about the causes of digestive disorders, such as gas, bloating, diarrhea, constipation, abdominal pain, belching, and acid indigestion. Then we can turn our attention to what you can do to help your body return to normal.

As with all health conditions, stress can make digestive problems worse. Stress causes all of the muscles in the entire body, including the colon, to contract. When muscles tighten, the blood supply and nerves leading to them are pinched. This reduces the flow of blood to the muscles and interferes with their nerve control. Most patients report that when they are under stress, especially mental or emotional stress, the symptoms of their digestive disorders are aggravated and accelerated.

The most common treatment for digestive discomfort due to heartburn or acid reflux is to suppress the symptoms with drugs. But using drugs to treat the discomfort can give you a false sense of security. Even though the symptoms may subside, the condition may still be progressing.

Traditional digestive discomfort medications generally reduce the body's production of stomach acids, which might provide temporary relief. However, the body needs stomach acid to digest food, so when the brain senses there is not enough stomach acid to properly digest food, it sends a message to produce more stomach acid, thus making the problem worse in the long run. And if you don't feel the symptoms of your digestive problems, you're probably going to be less cautious and do things that actually make your problems worse. Pain is not always a bad thing. It's sometimes an indicator there's a problem that needs to be fixed.

If you experienced an unrelenting muscle spasm in your leg, you would consider visiting a qualified doctor to treat, massage, and relax the muscle. Most folks are surprised to find that the same treatment is often very effective to relieve muscle spasms in your colon. I have found that abdominal massage and abdominal adjustments have helped treat the cause of many digestive disorders. In fact, this condition is so common that I often perform abdominal adjustments on 10–15 patients in a single day.

# Hiatal Hernia

Although many digestive conditions are caused by spasms of the colon, some have other origins. Many of my patients have a condition that causes the stomach to push up against the diaphragm, which is a sheet of muscle that divides the upper chest cavity from your abdomen and assists in the process of breathing. This pressure can cause the stomach to spasm, or in severe cases, actually push up through the diaphragm. This is called a hiatal hernia. Some medical experts estimate that more than half of all Americans over 60 suffer from this condition. Over half! And most don't even know it!

A diaphragm strain or hiatal hernia can cause acid reflux, sometimes called GERD (gastroesophageal reflux disease). To explain GERD further: the biggest and strongest muscle in your body is not the heart or the legs; it is your diaphragm, the muscle that separates the chest from the abdomen. It may not be a muscle that you think about much, unless you have trouble with it. It is rare for a doctor to diagnose a diaphragm strain or spasm, yet if we could find a quick, simple way to evaluate the diaphragm for normal function, we could avoid many unnecessary treatments based on improper diagnoses and save huge amounts of money spent on unnecessary drugs.

Many people carry around the damage and symptoms from a strained diaphragm for many years. Some even carry it around for a lifetime!

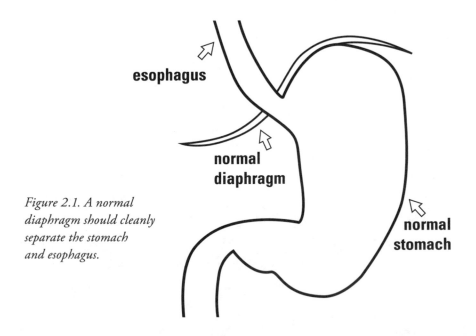

*Figure 2.1. A normal diaphragm should cleanly separate the stomach and esophagus.*

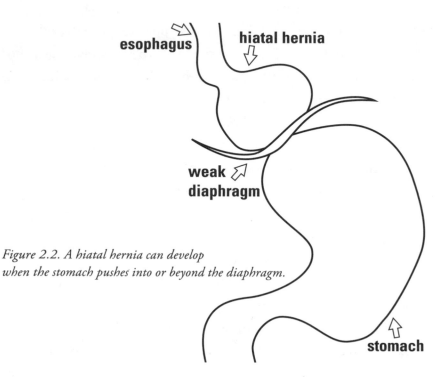

*Figure 2.2. A hiatal hernia can develop*
*when the stomach pushes into or beyond the diaphragm.*

Many of these people not only experience stomach and reflux problems, but they also experience heart and circulatory symptoms, all caused by weakness of the diaphragm. This condition is often missed by ordinary medical procedures as the problem may not be found even if an endoscope is put down into a patient's stomach. If a hiatal hernia or diaphragm strain is misdiagnosed, these folks can be treated with dangerous drugs for suspected stomach, heart, and circulatory problems.

So many doctors and patients fail to manage this problem correctly because they overlook the mechanics of the stomach. Some of my patients have a hiatal hernia diagnosis, but most do not. They are not even aware that it is possible for the stomach to actually move out of place. If they do know about the condition, most are certainly not aware that it is possible to reposition an internal organ for better digestive functioning.

## Repositioning for Relief

Most people think of their internal organs as being fairly stationary, but it is possible for organs to be positioned incorrectly. And that can cause major problems. I sometimes call this "squished stomach syndrome." That makes it pretty clear, right?

If properly diagnosed, the problem can be corrected by simply stretching the diaphragm back to its normal position, freeing the stomach from its trapped position, allowing normal breathing as well as normal stomach function. The entire diagnosis and treatment takes me less than two minutes.

If the stomach is in spasm, or if a hiatal hernia occurs, I employ a very simple technique to massage the stomach and pull it back to its normal position. I essentially pull the stomach away from the diaphragm and get the diaphragm to relax. If my arm was in spasm, what would I do? I'd massage it. If your stomach is in spasm, you massage it. Using this technique, the stomach can actually drop down to its normal position, allowing it to return to normal function, in many cases. Most people do not have any idea that this type of technique even exists!

Ask your chiropractor or your potential chiropractic office if they do "stomach adjustments." Trust me, if they don't, you'll know real "quick-like," as they say in the South!

# Inadequate Digestion

If food is not digested properly, it will stay in the stomach longer as the body attempts to digest the food more thoroughly. If it stays there too long, it will begin to putrefy, which can cause this "rotten" food to reflux back up the esophagus as the body tries to get rid of it. Or the food can stay in the digestive tract too long and produce excessive amounts of gas, bloating, or constipation.

Remember, the stomach's job is to break down proteins into amino acids. If the food is not broken down properly in the stomach, it can pass on to the small intestine in a partially digested state. If the stomach does not break down proteins into small enough pieces, the small intestine has a tough time trying to break them down into amino acids.

Some of the bigger chunks of protein can be absorbed into the body. The body does not recognize these bigger pieces of protein, so it sends out the immune system cells to attack them and get them out of the body. This can cause what is known as an allergic reaction. Symptoms may include sinus inflammation, runny nose, swelling, hives, rashes, other skin conditions, headaches, watery eyes, and diarrhea.

In addition, if the protein is not broken down correctly, not enough amino acids are produced to meet the body's requirements. Amino acids are utilized by the muscular system first; if there are any left, they will be sent to other parts of the body where they're needed for vital functions.

## Starving the Brain

The last place to get any "leftover" amino acids is in the higher cortical functions in the brain. Although the brain desperately needs these amino acids to bind with certain B vitamins to produce neurotransmitters, it gets the last shot at them. Doesn't seem right, does it?

When you eat protein, your stomach acids break it down into amino acids, and the amino acid tryptophan goes into your small intestine and combines with vitamin B6, which produces something called 5-HTP, which becomes serotonin, a neurotransmitter that helps your brain focus and relax, as we discussed earlier in this chapter.

But 95 percent of serotonin in the body is used by your digestive system and other parts of the body. By keeping the digestive system working well, you can make sure there is enough serotonin to go around so that the brain doesn't get shortchanged. As discussed above, many people who are diagnosed with anxiety disorders, clinical depression, or bipolar disorder are prescribed medications that boost serotonin. My thought is to try to produce more serotonin by fixing the digestive system! Novel concept, right?

If we look at people with psychological disorders, they often will have excessive amounts of flatulence, bloating, and belching, and are often ticklish, especially on the sides of their ribs. This ticklishness is the body's defense mechanism; it's protecting the digestive system, which is in distress. If you "attack" the area of the digestive system, the body protects itself by creating the sensation of being ticklish so that the patient pulls away and does not allow the "attacker" any closer access to the digestive system. Interesting, huh?

The latest research shows that many psychological disorders stem from malfunctions in the digestive system, where neurotransmitters are produced. An imbalance in neurotransmitters creates psychological disorders. Fix the gut and you fix the brain.

By the way, there now are scientific tests that measure the levels of neurotransmitters. Ask your doctor about them. If he or she is not familiar with this test, consult another until you find one who is familiar with them. Knowing your neurotransmitter levels is invaluable in helping to identify deficiencies.

# Brain, Spine, and Digestion

Also keep in mind the connection between your brain, spine, and digestion. Pinched nerves in the spine must be identified and corrected because if one of your spinal nerves that controls a portion of the digestive system is pinched, messages traveling from the brain down the spine and out to the nerves in the organ are not being transmitted properly. Therefore, the organ cannot function normally.

Misaligned bones in the spine cause most pinched nerves, and these nerves are the body components that control organ function. Studies have shown that the weight of a feather on a nerve can decrease its ability to transmit nerve impulses by as much as 80 percent! So imagine what a horrible impact a pinched nerve can have on your digestive system—not to mention your entire body!

The pinched nerve must be corrected so other forms of treatment can be fully effective. Although pinched nerves can produce a lot of pain, not all pinched nerves hurt. Ninety percent of your nerves do not transmit pain impulses, so you may not even be aware if you have a problem. Many of my patients have no idea that they have pinched nerves, nor do they ever associate their digestive problems with pinched nerves. Only a qualified chiropractor can determine if you have one and properly correct it.

### Other Conditions

There are many health conditions not directly addressed in this chapter that affect the digestive system. Some of the more severe problems include irritable bowel syndrome, Crohn's disease, and colitis. Symptoms of these conditions can include gas, bloating, diarrhea, and constipation. All of these symptoms are warning signs telling you something is wrong. Treating the symptoms might give you temporary relief, but treating the cause will help you achieve long-term healing.

By following *Dr. Joe's Secrets of Extreme Health*, you can achieve great results, and you'll be very happy to get your life back!

# Foods Can Irritate; Foods Can Heal

Certain foods can irritate a digestive condition. The foods that most often cause problems for my patients are dairy, wheat, barley, and rye—we will discuss those later. There are also other foods that might not be good choices for those who struggle with digestive problems. These include:

- Meat
- Eggs
- Citrus fruits
- Corn

- Spicy foods
- Vinegar (except for raw organic apple cider vinegar)
- Chocolate

- Yeast
- Coffee
- Soda (especially cola)
- Alcohol

The easiest way to determine if you are sensitive to a certain food is to totally avoid that single food for five days. On the sixth day, eat that food and see if you have a flare-up. If you begin to experience painful or problematic symptoms, you need to avoid this food in the future. Sometimes, after you eliminate the irritating foods and your digestive system heals, you can go back to eating some of these foods. However, you need to get your gut healed first.

Eating smaller meals can also help the digestive system to heal. Eat four to five small meals a day versus the typical three large meals per day. The meal (in physical size) should not be larger than your fist. We'll get into more specifics on what you should eat for these meals later in the book.

Now that you know some foods to avoid, you should also know there are foods that can help the digestive system heal.

# "Cauliflower is nothing but cabbage with a college education."
# —Mark Twain

For the most part, I recommend eating as many raw vegetables as you can, but only about three or four pieces of fruit a day, or about 25 grams of fructose, which is a sugar found in fruit. More about that later.

However, in some situations where digestive symptoms are more intense or painful, certain raw fruits and vegetables may actually cause discomfort. In these situations, continue to eat cooked fruits and vegetables, and slowly introduce a combination of raw fruit and vegetables into the diet. You can read more about this plan in my book *Eating Right for the Health of It!*

# The Salad Fix

Here's a really simple way for you to see if I'm for real or not. I want you to give me one day of your life. Have a salad for each meal on that day and see what happens. All I want is one day, a measly 24 hours.

Have a big salad for breakfast, a big salad for lunch, and a big salad for dinner. (If you can't eat raw veggies yet, choose three meals of steamed veggies that you *can* eat.) You can make your own salad dressing, quickly, easily and very inexpensively. Here's the recipe:

- Raw organic apple cider vinegar, 1 part
- Extra virgin olive oil, 2 parts
- Whatever seasonings you want, preferably organic

Use any type of lettuce, but bear in mind the darker the color, the greater the nutrition, so try to avoid iceberg. But if that's the only kind you have, use it. Even though iceberg may have little nutritional value, it is still better than eating a cheeseburger. Adorn your salad with celery, carrots, onions, broccoli, cauliflower, and any other vegetables you like.

You can do kale. You can do chard. You can do radish leaves. I once alarmed a date when I made a radish salad with the tops and the bottoms fresh from my garden. She said, "What are you doing? You can't eat radish tops!"

I explained to her that the radish tops are bitter and that bitter vegetables help to detoxify the liver. And she said, "Gosh, I would have cut them off and thrown them away!" I said, "Well, now you won't, now that you're educated about the beauty and value of radish tops!" So, in my book just about anything green is good.

During one of my recent lectures, a lady raised her hand and asked, "Dr. Joe, I hear what you're saying, but how long do you think it's going to take before I start seeing some changes?"

With the straightest face I could manage, I said, "I think it's going to take a while."

I paused. "It'll probably take about 24 hours." And then I stopped talking.

So, can't you just give me one day of your life and see if I'm telling the truth or not? I am. You'll feel it. Give me one day, no cheating. Just one day. Organically grown salads, that's it. Watch how you feel the next day. Watch how you feel that night. You'll be amazed.

I'm not lying to you. I get no benefit from lying to you. I don't own an organic salad greens shop. Everything I'm telling you is true, and if you don't believe me, just try it and see. If I'm wrong, so what, you eat well for one day.

But if I'm right, and I'm pretty sure I am, you will know what it feels like to eat healthy, you will have saved some money, and now you can decide if you would rather feel good or feel bad from now on.

# Dr. Joe's #2 Secret of Extreme Health:

## The Nervous System

s discussed in the previous two chapters, your digestive system plays a crucial role in your overall health. Another critical player—and another one you probably don't think about often—is your nervous system. Problems with your nervous system can short-circuit your energy, sap your vitality, and lower your ability to fight off disease.

The brain sends messages down the spine and out to the nerves in every cell in your body. There are about 80 trillion cells in your body, and every single one is controlled by the nervous system. So, if you have a bone in your spine that's out of place, a muscle spasm, a hip that is higher than the other, or a twisted spine, a pinched nerve could be blocking the messages from the brain to the body. You HAVE to make sure that your nervous system is working—and working well—if you want to obtain and maintain good health.

There are some simple tests you can take to see if you are suffering from some nerve interference. The easiest test is to ask yourself, "Do I have back or neck pain?" If you do, you have an irritated nerve. The best thing for this condition is to find out what is irritating the nerve and repair it.

Another way you can check to see whether your nervous system is working properly is to look in the mirror. Is one ear, shoulder, or hip, higher than the other? This misalignment can indicate an imbalance that could be putting pressure on nerves and blocking those critical messages from the brain to the rest of the body.

## Nerves and Your Spine: The Importance of Alignment

By far, the most common cause of back pain is a bone in the spine that has moved out of alignment. This is a simple issue that can usually be resolved through the relatively painless work of a chiropractor. I am stunned by the number of people who live their lives consumed by back and neck pain, some of whom even proceed to risky and needless back surgeries, without ever thinking to consult with a chiropractor.

I am not against surgery, but in many cases it is not necessary. If there is a more conservative approach, I would suggest you try that first. Chiropractic care is definitely worth a try before you proceed to heavy-duty prescription painkillers or a risky surgery.

I believe all doctors should work together for the health of their patients. I would love to see a world where all different types of doctors unite to teach their patients how to prevent and resolve negative health issues.

### The Role of Pain

Pain is as an indicator of a problem and can sometimes let you know that you need help for your nervous system. However, about 90 percent of your nerves don't perceive pain. For example, there is a nerve that goes to your pancreas, but you don't feel your pancreas work. There are nerves that go to your heart, lungs, liver, spleen, colon, gallbladder, toenails, and all of your other body parts and organs. If you don't experience sensations when these organs are working correctly, you also may not feel pain when they don't work. Just because you feel no pain doesn't mean you can ignore other signs related to the state of your health.

You may experience some symptoms if these organs are not working correctly, but sometimes the pain doesn't occur until the later stages of malfunction. By then, it might be too late to correct a problem or repair damage. A qualified practitioner can test the nerves that don't feel pain. So why risk it? Get a chiropractor to check you out.

## Chemical or Physical?

There are two main ways nerves malfunction: chemical and physical. Chemical factors include food, drugs, alcohol, and environmental toxins. We can chemically alter the function of a nerve. For example, when you get up to leave the bar after consuming a lot of alcohol, your brain may say, "Hey, feet, move so I can stay steady and not fall down." But your feet don't move, and you fall down. This miscommunication between your brain and your feet occurs because the alcohol gets into the part of the brain at the back of the skull called the cerebellum—the part of the brain that helps control balance. So, if we start poisoning the cerebellum with alcohol, the brain's ability to communicate with the feet is chemically altered.

The body is nothing but a sack of chemicals. We're not plugged into the wall, so we have to generate our own electricity to power our nervous system. How do we do this? By the chemicals we put in our own body.

In this way, our bodies are like a car battery. If you put good chemicals into a car battery, you produce a lot of electricity. If you don't put quality chemicals in a battery, you won't produce much. When you buy a cheap battery, it doesn't work very well, does it? My grandfather, who came from Germany, used to say to me, "Josef, always buy the best. It's always cheaper."

I never quite got what he meant when I was younger, but now I do. What he meant was this: if you spend the money up front for the best services, tools, whatever, you will save yourself money down the road when you don't have to replace, repair, or redo the damage done by the cheaper service or product.

Putting the proper chemicals in your body will make the nervous system work better. Sometimes it costs a little more to get those quality chemicals. But in the long run, it will actually save you money. It may also save your life. Or give you back the life you used to enjoy.

Physical malfunctions can also affect your nervous system. If a bone moves out of place, there is swelling, which compresses nerves and can affect the flow of messages from the brain to the body and back from the body to the brain. We call this situation a "pinched" nerve, although we should probably call it a "compressed" nerve. But I didn't make the rules, so I'm just going with pinched nerve here.

If a bone is out of place and pinching a nerve, wouldn't it make sense to just move the bone back into place so that the nerve can be freed up to function correctly? Call me crazy, but to me, this makes sense.

## Proper Function of the Nervous System

In order for the nervous system to function properly, it must have three things: stimulation, oxygen, and nutrition. Without all three of these, the body is incapable of functioning properly at 100 percent capacity. If you have a pinched nerve, that nerve is not providing the correct stimulation to the brain. This is why I sometimes have patients do particular exercises that are specifically designed to stimulate a certain part of the brain.

Now, let's talk about oxygen. You have to have oxygen for the brain to function. Most people don't breathe properly. Many folks don't breathe deeply enough because their stomach is out of place, pushing up against the diaphragm, not allowing it to drop down low enough to allow the person to take deep breaths. These deep breaths allow the lungs to take in enough oxygen to allow the brain to function optimally.

The fourth cervical nerve (that's the fourth one down from the top of your neck) is the phrenic nerve, which tells your diaphragm to go up and down. If you pinch or irritate that nerve, the diaphragm can't function properly, which can affect your ability to breathe. Other nerves also contribute to breathing, and they can also cause problems if they are being irritated.

You have to correct such problems. Massage the stomach away from the diaphragm and unpinch the phrenic nerve going to the diaphragm and the lungs themselves.

Good nutrition is also vital for the nerves, and it can also be beneficial in helping the body maximize oxygen intake. If you eat a lot of fatty foods, it can cause your red blood cells to clump together, which makes it hard for them to transport enough oxygen.

# "As the twig is bent, so grows the tree."
# —Alexander Pope

# Witness to Problems

As a practicing chiropractor, I see all types of accidents, injuries, and bad posture that contribute to a breakdown of the musculoskeletal system. The real danger in these types of injuries is that the nervous system becomes impaired. We've all held our breath as we've watched a professional athlete knocked unconscious on the playing field—or even worse—seen them carted off on a medical gurney, unable to move. Such injuries can lead to a breakdown in the signals from the brain. Many diseases are caused by or complicated by a nervous system that is not operating at 100 percent of its potential.

So are your twigs bent? Have you checked with a chiropractor who can make sure that your nervous system is operating at maximum effect to ward off disease, keep your mental capacities sharp, and help with those aches and pains from the injuries that you sustained during your weekend warrior days?

Being a chiropractor AND a nutritionist, I hear all sorts of complaints. Here are some of them:

- Back pain (not so shocking)
- Neck pain (not so shocking)
- Headaches (not so shocking)
- Digestive problems—gas, abdominal pain, bloating, diarrhea, constipation, cramping (are you telling me that a chiropractor can fix this?)
- Symptoms involving fibromyalgia (many patients tell me they didn't know there *were* treatments other than prescription drugs for this condition!)
- Sexual malfunction—like all organs, if you pinch a nerve in the sex organs, they can't work properly. A bad diet can compromise your circulation, and both men and women need that for normal sexual function!

# Fibromyalgia and Other Pain Issues

I have SO many patients who come to me with a diagnosis of fibromyalgia, which is a very painful condition. Most have been told that it is untreatable. I want to address this particular subject right now. Those of you who suffer from this condition will obviously want to pay close attention. However, even if you have not been diagnosed with fibromyalgia, these rules apply to you if you are in pain.

Symptoms of fibromyalgia include pain, fatigue, muscle aches, and lethargy. Many chiropractors and "nontraditional" doctors use an unusual method to identify this condition. A trained professional touches certain points on the shoulders, elbows, and other places; if a patient indicates that a certain number of these trigger points are sore when touched, fibromyalgia is diagnosed.

Many times in the case of fibromyalgia, traditional doctors treat the symptoms, but the *cause* is ignored. Again, I ask why we don't try to understand what causes the problem when we are considering treatment? With fibromyalgia—as with just about every disease known to man—I find that there are three conditions in the body that are not in balance: the nervous system, the digestive system, and nutritional levels.

For example, the nerves affected by fibromyalgia are essentially raw with irritation from nutritional and digestive issues, and they are especially aggravated by nervous system malfunctions such as pinched nerves. In my practice, some fibromyalgia patients literally scream in pain when we barely touch them for an adjustment or treatment. They usually say they feel almost all of the nerves in their body are just "raw."

## Treating Inflammation

What we need to do to treat fibromyalgia (and many other conditions as well) is to calm the body down, and the quickest way to do this is to make sure there is as little inflammation as possible in the body. Much inflammation is due to diet and environmental factors. Even if you are eating a good diet, chemicals in products like perfume, hair spray, commercial deodorants, and plug-in air fresheners can cause an inflammatory reaction in the body.

How many of you have noticed that being around someone wearing a lot of perfume can make your nose run? That is an example of an inflammatory reaction. You can see that clinical external reaction, but what you can't see is the internal inflammatory reaction that caused it.

# Flying Under the Radar

The word "clinical" means something is happening in your body and you're aware of it. A "subclinical" condition means something is happening in your body, but you're not aware of it.

A good example of a subclinical condition might be the onset of high blood pressure. You don't realize your blood pressure is high until you get it checked because you haven't felt any symptoms. Once you experience symptoms of high blood pressure, the condition is then considered "clinical," because your body has made you aware of an existing condition.

Many times, I find my patients have subclinical conditions that eventually manifest themselves as issues and become clinical later on.

## Inflammatory Diets

So, regarding fibromyalgia, I look at someone and ask, "What are you eating?" I've never had a patient with fibromyalgia who was following a good diet. I have to advise them to avoid the "inflammatory" foods—alcohol, meat, sugars, dairy, coffee, sodas, artificial sweeteners, breads, cookies, cakes, doughnuts, pastas. Sugar is a biggie in terms of causing inflammation—a huge contributing factor to raging inflammation in the body.

When it comes to nutrition, not just in dealing with fibromyalgia but with *all* nutritional conditions, many times it's not *what* you eat that can help you improve; it's what you STOP eating. Nutrition in most cases is passive, not active—you have to *not* do something to make it work.

Let me repeat that so I know you read it correctly. *You have to not do something to make it work.* For instance, you have to NOT consume alcohol, meat, sugars, dairy coffee, sodas, artificial sweeteners, breads, cookies, cakes, doughnuts, pastas.

After a "diet diary" review with my patients, I advise them to eat "anti-inflammatory" foods: a little bit of fruit, a lot of vegetables, some nuts, and some seeds. When I share this with my patients or my seminar attendees, many of them say, "Well, gosh, that's so limiting."

So here's a shortcut: if you wrote down everything that you've eaten for the past year, you'd recognize a pattern. You'd see about six or seven foods appear in your diet over and over again. Now take away those six or seven inflammation-producing foods and replace them with six or seven "good" foods. Problem solved. It's easier, it's cheaper, it's quicker than anything you're doing right now, and it's extremely effective in most cases.

*Adjusting the Nervous and Digestive Systems*

After providing diet advice to my fibromyalgia patients, we then look at the nervous system. Are any nerves pinched? Are bones out of place that can cause a nerve to become irritated and painful? If so, then we should put the bones back in place.

Then, we have to look at the digestive system, which is so often ignored in healthcare. When we look at fibromyalgia patients, we often find their digestive system is not working properly, and they're not assimilating their food properly. Most fibromyalgia patients are over-weight, and they experience gas, bloating, diarrhea, and constipation.

So, we do something that most treatment plans never include: we look at the stomach. Frequently we find that it is out of place, and then we take the stomach and massage it back to its normal position. Most people have never heard of this treatment.

The most difficult issue with many fibromyalgia patients is that they use food as comfort. It makes sense. They are in a LOT of pain, so they use food to psychologically help reduce the pain. *But the comfort food is causing the pain!*

We get our patients off the "comfort foods" and on to fruits and vegetables, nuts and seeds. Then we combine that change with our treatments to make sure the nervous and digestion systems are working properly and at maximum efficiency. Pain and inflammation will lessen!

# Choosing a Chiropractor

If you are suffering from any of the symptoms or conditions I've described in this chapter and have not tried chiropractic treatment, you should. Many people don't recognize how chiropractic treatments and adjustments can improve many different areas of health, especially the internal organ adjustments that can greatly speed up the process of correcting digestive issues. While I can't guarantee that a chiropractor can solve every problem, we can certainly help to get your nervous system operating at its maximum efficiency, which will help improve all of your other health issues.

People ask me all the time, "Dr. Joe, I don't live anywhere near you, so how can I find a good chiropractor?"

Here are some general tips for finding an effective chiropractor.

- Ask if the doctor performs "soft-tissue adjustments," which are adjustments of the internal organs, not just "neck and back" treatments. This is REALLY important! If the doctor or staff don't know how to answer that question, they most likely do not offer that type of adjustment.

- Ask how long the chiropractor has been in practice. You generally don't want an inexperienced mechanic to work on your car, and the same goes for your other ride—your body. You want to find an experienced professional who's doing such a great enough job that patients come to him for years and years. Bear in mind that there are many fine young doctors out there, but this is just a good general rule of thumb. I think it's interesting that a lot of chiropractors practice well into their 80s. What I have found is that for most chiropractors, their practice and their habits are a lifestyle—not just a job!

- Ask the chiropractor if she or he has ever seen cases like yours and how many. This will tell you how experienced the doctor is with your particular issues. If the chiropractor does not have a lot of experience dealing with your specific problem areas, you don't want to go there! Literally.

- If the chiropractor has had experience dealing with cases like yours, ask what kind of results have come from the typical treatment.

- If you are looking for a chiropractor and diet advice, ask if the doctor works with nutrition and has had training in that area. In my practice, I deal with both. I do adjustments, discuss nutrition, *and* I have an entire line of supplements I've developed to assist in nutritional health.

- Here's my number one suggestion when you are looking for a chiropractor: Ask your friends if they have a great chiropractor. Then contact that chiropractor and ask the questions listed above.

Always remember, *you* are hiring the doctor, not vice versa. Think of it as a job interview. Do your due diligence to determine if the chiropractor or other doctor will work out. If not, fire them! There are always plenty more doctors out there, and you have to find the doctor who fits you, not the other way around.

CHAPTER 5

# Dr. Joe's #3 Secret of Extreme Health:

## Nutrition and the Seven Deadly Sins

When I consult with my patients, I spend a lot of time educating them about what to eat—and what NOT to eat. Healthy eating habits are key to getting the right nutrition, and nutrition is one of the key building blocks to a healthy life. It sounds simple, right?

Think again, my friend. The world we live in today is vastly different from the one I grew up in. What you find at the supermarket is genetically modified food filled with chemicals, steroids, hormones, and antibiotics and depleted of nutrients. The changes in our food supply have forever changed the American diet.

Unfortunately, many Americans know very little about these changes. But you can no longer sit by as a passive observer in your own life. You must take charge of finding out about our food and then using all the knowledge available to you to create a better life for you and your family.

Many of my patients are flabbergasted when they learn the facts about what is "approved" as healthy food. Once they learn the truth, it changes their lives forever.

One of my good friends was the founder of one of the largest fast-food companies in the U.S. When he realized that what he was feeding people was hurting them, he sold the whole chain and opened up a healthy café in Atlanta.

I once had a patient, a fast-food restaurant employee, who came to me because of back problems. After I worked with her and educated her, she changed her eating and her lifestyle, and her pain was resolved. But I was shocked when she walked into my office one day and said, "I *have* to quit my job. I just can't, in good conscience, feed people the garbage we are feeding them in my restaurant anymore. I now know what they are really eating, and I just can't do it anymore."

So, you see, creating healthy eating habits is about more than just the foods we eat—it's about the way we live our lives. You cannot separate one from the other. Once you get this concept, you will change your whole viewpoint—just like my friend and my patient did.

# "Americans will eat garbage provided you sprinkle it liberally with ketchup."
## —Henry James

I'm going to try to keep this chapter humorous because some of the things I'm going to write about may upset some people. And I'm also going to recap some points I've already made so that you can see how everything fits together. Everything you need to know about nutrition will not fit into one chapter—you'll find more information in the following sections and scattered throughout the book. But this is where it starts.

# Seven Deadly Sins of Nutrition

I spend a lot of time talking about the Seven Deadly Sins. No, I have not become a priest. I'm talking about the Seven Deadly Sins of Nutrition that destroy our health.

People come to me and say, "Dr. Joe, I want to eat better. I want to lose weight. I want to feel better. I have depression. I have anxiety. What can I do to get better?" And I answer, "There are seven foods that you really need to consider limiting or totally eliminating from your diet: alcohol, meat, dairy, sugar, coffee, soda, artificial sweeteners."

(Tobacco would be the eighth sin, but if you smoke, you can pretty much ignore what I'm going to say anyway because it really doesn't matter. If you do smoke, please quit.)

So, those are the seven foods you need to NEVER put in your body. That leaves you 120,000 good foods to go wild over. Food is the one thing we are all exposed to and consume, usually several times a day. So, it's a good idea to consume foods that will help enhance all systems of the body or—at the very least—not weaken them.

Yes, I can hear you groaning from here! When you read my Seven Deadly Sins list, you said, "My gosh, that's my whole diet!" I'm a realist, folks, so I realize some of you won't do EVERYTHING I say in this book. That's okay. This is "brown belt" nutrition. (When you're ready to go "black belt," we'll need to sit and talk.) But do SOMETHING.

# More Foods to Avoid

I know you're still worrying about the seven things I've told you not to eat. Well, as long as you're worrying about it, I'm going to add a few more to the list—most of these already fall into one of the sinful categories, but sometimes it's helpful if I spell these out right up front so you know EXACTLY what I'm talking about:

- Breads
- Cookies
- Cakes
- Doughnuts
- White rice
- Pasta
- Refined foods
- Hydrogenated oils
- Most commercial canned soups
- Potato chips
- Margarine
- Most commercial cereals
- Nuts roasted in oil
- Commercial peanut butter
- Fruit in heavy syrup (canned peaches, pineapples, etc.)
- Foods that contain nitrates, nitrites, sulfates, and sulfites (nonorganic dried fruit, certain pickled foods, wine)
- Most commercial crackers
- Steroids (specifically animal products that may have been injected with steroids)
- Hormones
- Antibiotics
- Many food additives, colorings, pesticides, herbicides, and some "natural" flavors

## *Dr. Joe's general rule of healthy eating: If you can't pronounce it, don't eat it!*

When you make one little change, you'll say, "Gee, that wasn't so hard." And then you'll be ready to make another little change. And another little change. Then start looking for some subtle improvements in your life. You might notice that you sleep better, go to the bathroom better, have a better love life, have more energy, or your life overall just starts getting better. When it does, you'll know why.

# "If man made it, don't eat it!"
## —Jack LaLanne

Every one of these Seven Deadly Sins of Nutrition could be an entire book unto itself. However, I'm just going to touch on the highlights of each in this chapter.

## Alcohol

All jokes aside from your college days, alcohol really does kill brain cells. Do I need to explain this any further? Who out there is smart enough to stumble through life stomping their brain cells to death on a daily basis?

Alcohol destroys brain cells. Your brain controls what? Everything. There are about 80 trillion cells in your body, and every one of them is connected to your brain in one way or another. Alcohol dehydrates your body, damaging cells it doesn't kill, even causing wrinkles. It causes liver and pancreas malfunction. It also puts an extra burden on the organs that detoxify your body, preventing them from doing their regular jobs, and wearing them out.

Alcohol is also a diuretic. Simply put, it makes you urinate more. Did you ever notice that when you drink one beer, you pee out three? Where did those other two beers come from? Your body is giving up its own fluids—and guess what else is in that fluid? Precious vitamins, minerals, and nutrients. Your body is giving up its own vital fluids to flush the alcohol out of your system because if the alcohol gets to the brain, it destroys cells and those brain cells control everything. Your body's pretty smart! It's protecting itself and its control center.

So now you're dehydrated from drinking alcohol. What did I say early on? As we get older, our hunger and the thirst centers grow together so you're not as thirsty as you used to be. So you probably started out dehydrated even before you began drinking. The more you drink, the more you dehydrate. And then your brain shrinks. And then you wake up the next morning and wish you had never woken up. The dreaded hangover.

So, for your long-term health, alcohol is not the drink of choice—that's what I'm telling you.

In addition, when alcohol is digested it's converted into sugar. Some studies have shown that the consumption of alcohol diminishes the body's ability to burn fat, which is why, even if you drink "lite" beer, you are likely to develop a "beer belly." You are interfering with your ability to burn off fat.

Alcohol also lowers your testosterone level, which causes you to gain weight. Testosterone helps build muscle mass and is your sex-drive hormone. (And I'm talking boys AND girls here.) Studies show that testosterone levels can decrease by as much as 25 percent after a blood-sugar spike, which can come after drinking alcohol. When testosterone drops, so does something else.

## A Bottle of Red

But some of you are thinking, "I heard that a glass of red wine is good for your heart—everybody knows that." Everywhere I speak all over the world, people know that. It's actually true. A glass of red wine *is* good for your heart.

There is a component in red wine called resveratrol, which has been shown to actually help slow down the aging process. The problem is that only *organic* wine has any significant amount of resveratrol in it because nonorganic wine is sprayed with fungicides. The reason grapes produce resveratrol is to prevent fungi from doing damage. So, if we spray fungicides on the grapes, there's no fungus, and if there's no fungus, there's no resveratrol. So there's very little, if any, resveratrol in nonorganic wines.

Even more disappointing, it's not really the wine that's good for your heart—it's the red. It's the antioxidants and proanthocyanidins in the grapes. There's a big word, huh? And you don't even know if I spelled it right! I could be making that up, and I could be lying through my teeth to impress you with my big college word—but I'm not.

The darker the color of the fruit or vegetable, typically the more nutrients it has. So, red wine and dark-colored fruits and vegetables have lots of good stuff in them—stuff that's good for your heart. But you don't have to drink wine to get that good stuff.

Now, does the alcohol help to relax you? Yes, it does. However, any benefit that the alcohol is giving you is being negated by the drawbacks I discussed above. So, if you want to maximize the benefits of a glass of red wine, just drink a glass of grape juice. Or eat organic grapes. There's an idea! Just eat grapes. By the way, you would have to drink several bottles of organic wine a day to get any significant amount of resveratrol in your diet!

# Just a Little Bit of Brain Damage

I love it when my patients say, "But Dr. Joe, I don't drink, except on Wednesdays. We'll go out for margaritas during football season. Well, that and Fridays sometimes, but other than that I never drink." It cracks me up. Every time. These are the same folks that hang out with the 15 percent of my patients who swear they never have any digestive problems.

A little bit of alcohol? A little bit of brain damage. A lot of alcohol? A lot of brain damage.

So we're going to go out for a margarita, you and I, and it's going to destroy part of my brain that—generally speaking—controls my pancreas. So now the messages from the brain aren't being generated at 100 percent to control my pancreas. So then what happens? My pancreas is not working at 100 percent capacity.

Then we go out another time and I destroy a part of my brain that controls my spleen, my liver, and my gallbladder. And now those organs are not working at 100 percent. And so on. And so on.

You know the beer commercials that feature "the most interesting man in the world?" You'll notice they don't say "the smartest man in the world"!

---

## Dr. Joe's Brown Belt Suggestions to Cut Alcohol Consumption

Sometimes my clients and patients come to me, hat in hand, and are very honest with me. They'll say to me something like this: "Dr. Joe, I know what you're saying is true. I know I need to do what you're telling me to do, but it's just too hard for me to stop eating sugar and drinking alcohol, and to eat all those fruits and vegetables and nuts and seeds."

Trust me. I get it. I still miss my meatball subs. That doesn't mean I still eat them. But sometimes I do miss them. Hey, I'm Italian, what do you expect? Bad habits are challenging to break. So I'm going to give you some "brown belt suggestions" that can help you avoid the Seven Deadly Sins and establish healthier habits. These will help ease you into some new lifestyle habits that will eventually help you stop the bad habits entirely.

If you HAVE to drink alcohol, follow this rule: For every one drink you have, drink three glasses of water.

Why? Two reasons:

1. You'll be peeing all night, so you won't have time to drink very much!
2. It will prevent you from dehydrating as much.

And if you can get organic alcohol, give yourself bonus points!

Start with these brown belt training tips, and soon you'll find yourself drinking less and less—and feeling better and better.

# Meat

Whenever I discuss this subject, invariably someone snickers and brings up Elvis' supposed 50-pound colon. (Believe it or not, one of Elvis' most trusted confidants was named Joe Esposito. It wasn't me; just a small, useless fun fact for you!) I am not an Elvis colon expert, but I can tell you is this: meat can lie in your colon for three days or more, giving off carcinogenic gases.

In general, meats are highly acidic foods that rob your body of calcium, which can lead to osteoporosis and other degenerative diseases because your body uses calcium and other nutrients to neutralize acids. Meat purchased in a regular grocery store is usually loaded with chemicals, steroids, hormones, and antibiotics, which cause or contribute to many health problems, including weakening your immune system.

Our digestive system is designed more like that of herbivores (plant eaters) than of most carnivores (meat eaters). We don't have the teeth or the jaw design to adequately rip raw flesh off animals. Ever watch "Shark Week"? You'll know what I'm talking about if you have.

A carnivore's digestive system is relatively short. A carnivore will eat meat, swallow it essentially whole, and sleep for about 20 hours a day. The human digestive system is long and convoluted, which is the way a herbivore's digestive system is designed.

The number one consumer of your body's energy is sex. Digestion is number two; like sex, digestion is exhausting for the body. And meat is the most difficult substance for your body to digest. If you eat meat, you feel it. You get tired. It's exhausting to eat meat.

A carnivore sleeps for 20 hours a day because it takes so much energy to digest meat! But meat in a true carnivore's stomach is broken down relatively quickly and passed out. This process doesn't happen that quickly in our digestive systems.

It takes about 72 hours—three days—for a human body to completely digest meat. Why? Our bodies are just not designed to eat or digest meat efficiently.

# Meat Check

Now, let's say that today is Sunday. So that burger that you had on Thursday is still there, lying in your colon—and it's rotting. And when meat rots at 98.6 degrees for three days, what does it smell like? All together now: "**Eww.**"

Try this experiment: Take a piece of meat, put it in a cooler with no ice, close the lid, leave it outside at 98.6 degrees. Come back in three days.

What happens? The meat rots, and it stinks. Even worse, in your cooler, you might have visitors. You might have parasites, maggots, and worms.

Now if your freezer or cooler is sealed, and nothing gets in or out, where'd they come from? They're in the meat! And you eat the meat! Why do you do that?

# EEEEWWWW!

As I mentioned above, meat is an acid that robs your body of calcium. Study after study has shown that the more animal products you consume, the higher the rate of osteoporosis, because there are two amino acids in meats and dairy products called methionine and cysteine, which are acids the body has to neutralize. In order to do this, it has to use the precious calcium it needs to do other things like protect and strengthen your bones.

## More Stomach-Churning Facts about Meat

Hang on to your stomachs. It's going to be a bumpy read.

American animals raised for meat consume more than 30 million pounds of antibiotics a year. Most supermarket meat today comes from operations that routinely feed animals low doses of antibiotics; about 80 percent of all antibiotics used in the U.S. goes to farm animals. This constant ingestion of drugs helps bacteria learn how to outsmart the meds, creating dangerous strains of hard-to-kill "superbugs." These are in the meat you eat.

When people need antibiotics, they have to go to a licensed professional. But anyone can walk into a farm store and purchase pounds and pounds of antibiotics.

MRSA is a type of bacteria that doesn't respond to antibiotics. It kills more people than the AIDS virus and it's in your meat. Researchers have found that a good portion of the U.S. supermarket meat sampled contained staph infection bacteria, including the hard-to-kill and potentially lethal MRSA.

Sad chickens? In 2012, Johns Hopkins University did a study on the feathers of imported chickens to find out what the birds ingested before slaughter. Ready for this? Antidepressants. Painkillers. Antibiotics and allergy medication that have been banned for humans. And—in about 50 percent of the samples—caffeine. Why? Caffeine keeps chickens awake so they can eat more and grow faster.

And it's not just chickens. The USDA has also discovered traces of harmful veterinary drugs and heavy metals in U.S. beef—including animal wormers, penicillin, arsenic, and copper.

## Dr. Joe's Brown Belt Suggestions to Cut Meat Consumption

You may have no problem eliminating meat from your diet after what you've just read. But if you're still struggling, here are my suggestions to help you cut back—or quit altogether.

If you must eat meat, eat organic meat, and this goes for all animal products such as eggs. An organic label means the animal has not consumed or been injected with any steroids, chemicals, hormones, antibiotics, pesticides, herbicides, and/or tranquilizers, and they were ONLY fed an organic diet. This means that cows did NOT consume grain, which most cows do when they are raised for meat production. Organically raised cows eat grasses, which they are biologically designed to eat.

If you're going to eat fish, make sure it is wild, not farm raised. It'll have higher nutritional value and substantially fewer toxins. How can you know if it's a wild fish? It's the one wearing the party hat! Ha-ha! But seriously, folks, look for labels that say "wild caught." If it doesn't say that, chances are it's farm raised.

When Moses wrote the book of Leviticus (in the Christian Bible and Jewish Torah) long ago, he said not to eat shellfish. The water was a heck of a lot cleaner then than it is now, so I'd strongly advise staying away from all shellfish: lobster, shrimp, crab, clams, mussels, oysters, etc.

If you must eat meat, make sure your portion is no bigger than the size of the palm of your hand. Animal products have no fiber, so make sure you eat plants along with your meat so that the meat will not sit in your colon as long.

Some folks think white meat, such as chicken, pork or turkey, is better than red meat. Contrary to popular belief, pound for pound, both contain about the same amount of cholesterol, and both are still hard for your body to digest. Eat organic animal products to help lessen the amount of chemicals in your meat. Other than that, there really appears to be no "lesser evil" between white and red meat.

Meat. It's what's for dinner. Not so much. Not anymore.

# Monster Milk

Now let's just assume you can find a cow that ate nothing but organic grass, was happy and lived on a stress-free farm, was always in a good mood. If you milked that cow, you would get pure milk, not the pasteurized, homogenized, processed milk you find in stores today.

Maybe some of you are old enough to remember drinking milk as a kid that had something in it you don't find in milk today. What was that called? Flavor. That milk had flavor in it—and cream. Remember that? The cream would separate on top, and you scooped the cream off and left the milk on the bottom because that's where the good stuff was. I remember that. The milkman used to deliver it. Back then milk also had something else: nutrition.

But then we took out the good stuff. We started feeding cows diets they're not designed to eat. Instead of grass, cows today usually are fed genetically modified corn and soybeans. If left to their own devices, cows won't eat corn and soybeans.

Cows are born placid ruminants, but the feedlot factory farms increase their protein and fat intake in order to increase their milk output. They take them out of pastures full of the grass that cows have eaten for millennia, and incarcerate them in filthy stalags and force them to consume feed that may contain bovine blood and even chicken manure. And you thought corn and soybeans were bad! You might have read that bovine spongiform encephalopathy, better known as "mad cow disease," is transmitted by feeding cattle the by-products of infected cows.

This is why it is absolutely necessary to sterilize—pasteurize—milk these days. But pasteurization involves heating a substance at a very high temperature, and when you do this, you destroy a lot of the vitamins, minerals, and nutrients in it.

# Dairy

Dairy causes more allergic reactions in people than any other food. Commercial dairy products cannot be properly digested by humans due to the protein and sugars in them that we are not capable of breaking down. Milk changes its chemical structure when it is pasteurized. Many calves are fed pasteurized milk to kill pathogens in waste milk, and it doesn't help the calves to develop normally. Some calves that are fed pasteurized milk would need to get fed medication to live a normal life.

So much for milk doing a body good. Boy, marketing departments at dairies have outdone themselves on this one. Okay, I'm off on my rant on dairy, so hang on tight.

First of all, cow's milk is made for what? Baby cows. Any baby cows reading this book? In nature, when does a calf stop drinking milk? When it becomes an adolescent cow, I guess. When do most humans stop drinking milk? Never! And it's cow's milk—the milk of another mammal.

Our digestive systems are a lot different than baby cows' digestive systems.

## Mucus and Magnesium

When you drink milk, what happens? It creates mucus. Where does it create mucus? In your sinuses, obviously. But mucus can be building up in your lungs or your throat, as well. Do you know people who have to clear their throats all the time? Annoying, right? I know PLENTY of them, but once they got off dairy they quit having to do that. All their lives, they thought that's just how they were, but it turns out that's how they were *when they consumed dairy!*

And how about your colon? Or other organs? Even your reproductive system is composed of mucus membranes. Some women struggling with infertility have found that leaving off dairy products may make their ovum more approachable—in other words, not surrounded by a mucus slick.

I've been saying all along that you've got to be able to absorb your nutrients. It's not what you *ingest*, it's what you *digest*. Mucus buildup can cause all that good food you're putting into your body to just slide on through, leaving no souvenirs of nutrients behind. So, if your colon is clogged with mucus, it will adversely affect your digestion.

When you consume milk, butter, cheese, yogurt, or anything that comes out of a cow, you can increase your production of mucus. Pretty simple. And if you drink pasteurized milk (and about 99 percent of milk consumed in America today is pasteurized), you can only utilize a small percentage of the calcium that's in milk anyway. Most of the rest of it is chemically bound to casein once it's pasteurized, and we lack the ability to produce enough of the enzyme rennin to break down casein properly.

So you don't get a whole lot of usable calcium from drinking pasteurized milk. Plus, milk has proteins that are acids, which need to be neutralized, and the body uses calcium as one of its primary neutralizing agents. The net effect is that you can lose more calcium than you gain by consuming dairy products. Talk about a catch-22!

And there's a great study called "The Harvard Nurses' Health Study," where scientists followed about 100,000 nurses (and their eating habits) for more than 20 years. And they found—get ready for this one—that the more dairy products the nurses consumed, the higher the incidence of osteoporosis in nurses.

Now, let me get this straight. We humans have been told that we need to drink milk to get calcium into our bodies. But in this nurses' study, one thing that stands out is that the more dairy product these nurses consumed, the higher their incidence of osteoporosis.

To complicate matters even further, you can't absorb and utilize calcium well unless you have magnesium. How much magnesium does milk have? Almost zero. So even if everything I told you about milk was a lie (and it's not), it's been scientifically proven that you couldn't get the calcium you need from milk because you don't have any magnesium—unless you're consuming milk with something that has magnesium in it.

Magnesium comes from a plant-based diet—nuts and seeds mainly. Most people eating a meat- and dairy-based diet aren't eating the fruits, vegetables, grains, nuts, and seeds they need. Did you know that plants actually have calcium in them? Maybe not, because there is no American Plant Council to buy ads telling us, "Plants do a body good."

## Cheese

If drinking milk were not bad enough, we mess things up even further when we take out some of the water after we pasteurize and homogenize the milk we got from the cow that ate the bad food. That's how we create a thing called cheese.

Cheese. Whose idea was this? Let's take milk, add acid to it, let it rot, and let's eat it! I think we can blame the French for this idea.

Have you ever stopped to think about what causes the blue in bleu cheese dressing? It's mold! You wouldn't scrape your toilet bowl or your slimy shower or tub and put it on crackers, would you? But we take cheese, add mold, and then serve it at swanky parties.

Can't you just hear the cocktail party conversation? "Mmm. This is good. It's from France. It's French mold. It's more expensive than American mold. This is good mold!"

And how about yellow cheese? Where does that come from? Cows with jaundice?

# Non-Spoiler Alert

Worse than cheese is artificially processed cheese food spread. What is that? Is there anything else that you eat that has to have the word "food" in it to give you a heads-up? There wasn't a cow in the room when that stuff was made. This rubbish never goes bad. Even in a nuclear holocaust. Okay, I'm not really sure about the nuclear holocaust thing, but I'll betcha!

Here's a rule regarding food in general. Take it home with you. If it doesn't go bad, don't eat it. That's a good rule. You've seen those immortal hamburgers on the Internet, right? When it comes to fast food, I won't have what she's having.

"If it doesn't go bad, don't eat it." Put that on a T-shirt and a bumper sticker. Sell it down on the boardwalk.

## *Hormones and Antibiotics*

About 40 percent of the U.S. cows that give us milk are injected with something called recombinant bovine growth hormone, commonly reduced to its acronym, RBGH. What does it do? It causes a cow to produce more milk than it's supposed to. Two to three times more. What's the big deal, you ask? America's all about bigger and better, right?

Ladies, some of you may have kids, right? Remember when you were breastfeeding? How sore your "girls" were? Now, imagine "the girls" two to three times bigger. Ouch! And then when the hormones increase a cow's milk production, the udders can become engorged and rip and tear. Mothers out there who have experienced a breast infection will remember how much that hurts!

So what happens to cows with breast infections? Torn udders allow blood *and* the infection to drip into the milk that will then be shipped to market. But we can't have unlimited amounts of blood and pus in our milk, can we? No, we can't. That's why the government has a rule about this. I'm not kidding you. Producers can include no more than 750,000 somatic cells and/or blood cells in about eight drops of milk.

All together now: *EEEEEEWWWW*!

So what do we give the cow to conquer the infection that was enhanced by the hormones we gave the cow? Antibiotics. Eighty percent of antibiotics made in this country are made for animals, not for humans.

But we get the "benefits" of "better living through chemistry" because we get to eat the cow and drink the milk. Not so much. Because we're also getting the cow's antibiotics in our system, which are slowly making our immune system weaker and weaker while making the bugs in our bodies stronger and stronger.

## Brown Belt Suggestions to Cut Dairy Consumption

I'm hoping that 100% of you gave up milk while reading this yucky section. Milk—does it do the body good?

But if you are going to consume dairy, here are my suggestions.

Animal milk must be organic—and preferably raw—if you are going to drink it. Otherwise, look for substitutes. The good news is that there are plant-based substitutes for everything in the dairy world.

You can enjoy rice milk, coconut milk, almond milk, hemp milk, cashew milk, and quinoa milk. More and more "big box" grocery stores are beginning to carry these types of products, as their "natural sections" grow larger and larger each week.

There are even delicious plant-based alternatives for butter, yogurt, ice cream, cheese, and anything else that would normally come out of a cow!

With any of these products, I would suggest that you start small and work up to making them a bigger and bigger part of your diet. For example, if you are a big consumer of milk, try almond milk on your cereal as your first trial run. Eventually, you'll find that you prefer the plant-based products over milk. My patients often tell me that they are amazed at how bitter and acidic dairy milk tastes after they have been drinking plant-based milks for a while.

However, do be careful of the sugar content in the plant-based milks. Try to consume the ones with the lower sugar amounts. Which brings us to our next Deadly Sin.

# Sugar

The average American ingests 130 POUNDS of added sugars annually. Researchers are beginning to see the strange ways this overload of sugar is affecting people.

Here are 11 weird things that "sugar overload" is doing to your body:

1. Sugar makes your organs fat.
2. Sugar primes your body for diabetes.
3. Sugar surplus contributes to heart disease and strokes.
4. Sugar creates tense blood vessels, putting you on the path to high blood pressure, which ultimately makes a stroke or heart attack more likely.
5. Sugar may promote high cholesterol by sparking your liver to churn out more bad cholesterol while inhibiting your body's ability to clear it out.
6. Sugar surplus leads to Alzheimer's.
7. Sugar surplus turns you into a sugar junkie. It IS an addiction.

8. Regularly eating too much sugar interferes with your body's ability to tell your brain that you're full, leading you to eat more.

9. The sugar spike and crash compels you to consume even more sugar.

10. If you consume a lot of sugary junk food, you're more likely to develop depression.

11. Excess sugar consumption leads to wrinkles, saggy skin, and deactivated natural antioxidant enzymes because of "advanced glycation end" products (nicknamed AGEs).

Contrary to popular belief, sugar does not give you energy; it actually makes you weaker. Sugar is an acid, which robs your body of calcium and other nutrients as you digest it. Remember the sensation of cotton candy on your tongue? It was hot, right? Just think of that same chemical reaction scorching your liver, your kidneys, your heart, and your eyes. Reactions to sugar can cause sharp mood swings and alter personality. Improper sugar intake contributes to obesity because of its addictive nature.

# Sweet, Sweet Soda

How much sugar is in a can of soda? Any idea? A lot. Nine to twelve teaspoons, on average. If I were to take nine teaspoons of sugar and dump them down your throat, you'd think you were in a diabetic coma. Nine teaspoons—that's a lot of sugar. And yet every time we drink a can of soda, nine teaspoons of sugar. Yeah, I know, I'm doing it again—that repeating thing of mine. Nasty habit, eh? But not as nasty as the soda habit.

So, you're thinking to yourself, "But Dr. Joe, that's why I drink diet soda." That's why you drink diet? I'm going to get there, don't worry.

So sugar is an acid. When you put acid in your body, your body has to neutralize the acid. Acids are like Pac-Man. Remember Pac-Man, the video game? Like Pac-Man, acids like to eat through things. Your body has to neutralize these acids in self-defense, and as we saw previously, the body turns to calcium to neutralize acids. Study after study after study shows that one of the major causes of osteoporosis is not, Not, NOT too little calcium! It's too much acid!

In most cases, we don't need more calcium. We need less bad acid. If we cut back on our acids, the body doesn't have to utilize the calcium to neutralize the acid—and hey, we got lots of calcium left.

Sugar is not just empty calories—it also weakens the immune system. If you put white sugar in your body, your body has to give up nutrients to digest and break down the sugar. Most people don't understand the effect sugar has on white blood cells, which support your immune system by attacking invaders in the system. A normal white blood cell should destroy 14 bacteria (or germs) in its lifetime.

If you consume 24 teaspoons of sugar, or about the equivalent of two cans of soda, that same white blood cell will only be able to destroy one bacterium. This effect on the immune system can last for up to five hours. That is a 40 percent decrease in the immune system's ability to destroy bacteria! Not good! Especially when we know that the typical American consumes 52 teaspoons of sugar a day.

Another disgusting fun fact about sugar: as it is processed, it needs to be filtered to make it pretty and white. A charcoal filter is used. Some charcoal filters are made from charred animal bones. So for all you vegetarians out there, this is something to consider!

## High Fructose Corn Syrup

Another form of sugar that's even worse than plain white sugar is high fructose corn syrup (HFCS for short). HFCS is generally made with genetically modified (GMO) corn. Your body considers genetically modified corn a new protein unlike any we humans have typically been exposed to. Since your body doesn't recognize these foreign proteins, your immune system can actually attack these new substances. In fact, your immune system gets so excited, it can actually attack itself and can cause an autoimmune reaction that ranges from uncomfortable to life-threatening.

## Sinful and Acidic

What are the most acidic foods?

1. Alcohol
2. Meat
3. Sugar
4. Dairy
5. Coffee
6. Soda
7. Artificial sweeteners

There are those Seven Deadly Sins again!

Your body's immune system is NOT designed to attack itself, but these unnatural substances can cause it to get a little crazy. Some examples of autoimmune diseases are rheumatoid arthritis (RA) and lupus. RA generally attacks the joints, but lupus can be like WWIII all over your body—inside and out.

So, of course, the next question you want to ask is: if we change the diet, will rheumatoid arthritis or lupus go away? While I can't promise that this will happen 100 percent of the time, any time you can calm down the immune system, you will probably see amazing results. I have with my patients.

If you have a normally functioning nervous system, a healthy immune system, and good digestion, *everything in your health world will improve!*

Many studies have indicated that GMOs are actually dangerous to fertility and digestion, and may even be linked to cancer. So, I strongly urge you to stay away from any genetically modified foods, especially high fructose corn syrup.

GMO + HFCS = **BAD** (That's all the chemistry you need to know, folks!)

HFCS also suppresses the production of leptin, a hormone produced in the stomach to send messages to your brain to tell you that you feel full. HFCS does NOT suppress the production of grehlin, the hormone produced in your intestines to tell your brain that you're hungry.

Do you see where I'm going with this? HFCS stores more calories as fat than sugar does; it keeps you from feeling full and actually produces more of the hormone that makes you feel hungry. This is a bad combo all the way around.

Where do you find high fructose corn syrup? Just about everywhere. Read the labels on your food, and you'll be surprised where HFCS shows up.

So, in short, sugar is bad for you. High fructose corn syrup is even worse. And if you think that's bad, just wait until we get to artificial sweeteners!

### Dr. Joe's Brown Belt Suggestions to Cut Sugar Consumption

Look at your "sugar behavior" and view it as an actual addiction. This change in perspective will help you modify your behavior. Addicts in rehab programs are not allowed "a little bit" of alcohol, drugs, gambling, or whatever. Think of your sugar addiction in the same way. If you have just a "little treat," you set off the pleasure centers of your brain and you want more. You've got to have more. You're setting yourself up to fall off the wagon.

In order to wean yourself off the sugar, you can use stevia, which is a natural sweetener that is 300 times sweeter than sugar in its natural form. Sometimes stevia is mixed with maltodextrin, which might be made from GMO corn. So if you can get pure stevia, that's your best choice. But be careful—it's extremely sweet. One teaspoon of pure stevia would be like eating 300 teaspoons of sugar. That's why they cut it with the maltodextrin to dilute it. Many of my patients comment that stevia sometimes has a slightly bitter aftertaste. Some companies try to extract the bitterness, and the jury's still out on whether or not that's harmful.

If you want to grow your own stevia, it's pretty easy. It looks like a mint plant and can grow indoors or out. You take the leaves, dry them out, and then crush them. These leaves will be twice as sweet as sugar.

Organic maple syrup could be another alternative. It's not just for pancakes anymore! Make sure it's organic and labeled "grade B," which means it is taken out of the tree at the end of the season and has a higher nutritional value. If you use it, do so very sparingly—no more than two tablespoons a day.

Honey is another alternative sweetener, but it needs to be local and raw. Some commercial honey comes from bees that are fed high fructose corn syrup. I caution my patients and listeners to be careful with honey because it has a high fructose level. Honey has equal parts fructose and glucose but also contains antioxidants and vitamins. Darker colored honey contains more antioxidants than lighter colored honey.

Agave can contain more fructose than HFCS, so it's not really something I recommend, although a lot of "natural folks" out there do. Rice syrup is another alternative, but I'll level with you: it's not very sweet.

Just remember that breads, cookies, cakes, doughnuts, pastas, and anything else made with refined, processed grains (white flour, white sugar, etc.) break down into sugar.

# Coffee

Now I know this section is going to be hard for some of you to swallow.

Coffee beans are almost always contaminated with mycotoxins, damaging compounds created by molds, which grow on coffee beans (among other things). These compounds can cause all sorts of health problems like cardiomyopathy, cancer, hypertension, kidney disease, and even brain damage. They also make your coffee taste bitter, like it needs sugar.

Some types of coffee have more mycotoxins than others, which is why you see some studies showing a benefit to drinking coffee and others showing negative health outcomes. The problem is not just with the coffee, it's the mold on your coffee. It can even vary by individual batch, especially for large coffee producers.

Dave Asprey, in his article "Why Bad Coffee Makes You Weak," discusses the frightening stats regarding the amount of mycotoxins that are found in most low-quality brands of coffee. One study cited in this article showed that 91.7 percent of green coffee beans were contaminated with mold. This is before they were processed, which allows even more mold to grow. Another study showed 52 percent of green coffee beans and almost 50 percent of brewed coffees are moldy. Coffee is by far one of the largest sources of mycotoxins in the food supply.

Other researchers have noted that regular coffee consumption may contribute to exposure of humans to Ochratoxin A (OA). OA is bad news. It hits your kidneys, causes cancer, and messes up your immune system. Ochratoxin-generating mold is the type of toxic mold that can cause some serious damage to immune function and the autonomic nervous system.

## *Not an Energy Boost*

Contrary to popular belief, coffee doesn't give you energy. Adenosine receptor sites are located in the brain, and your brain builds up a supply of adenosine. Drinking coffee blocks these adenosine receptors. And let me explain why. The chemical adenosine that's released in your brain is absorbed at specific receptor sites, and when adenosine binds to receptors, brain activity slows down and you feel tired.

Simply put, adenosine helps you get sleepy and also dilates, or opens up, your blood vessels to make sure you're getting a good amount of oxygen to your brain when you sleep. Caffeine can block your adenosine receptor sites so the adenosine is not absorbed properly, which means you don't get tired.

Caffeine also causes your pituitary gland to secrete hormones that cause your adrenal glands to produce adrenaline. The increased production of adrenaline will keep you awake and give you a burst of energy. This is exactly why you drink coffee. You drink it to give you a burst of energy.

But your body is smarter than you. The body now starts producing more adenosine receptor sites to try to absorb more adenosine so that you can rest. The body does a lot of healing when it is at rest. Now that you have more adenosine receptor sites, you have to take in more caffeine to try to stop yourself from getting tired. Essentially, you build up a tolerance to caffeine. If it used to take you one cup of coffee to get that burst of energy, it now may take two, or three, or five, or 10. This is why so many people use caffeine on a daily basis.

Many people will have symptoms—especially headaches—if they try to eliminate caffeine from their diet. Here's a little trick for you to get over your caffeine addiction. Take a cup of plain black coffee and leave it on your desk; drink one tablespoon of that coffee every hour. This limited amount will help slowly return your brain to its normal functions while helping you avoid the headaches and other physical ailments many people feel when they give up their caffeine.

Like many addicting substances, caffeine increases the production of dopamine in your brain. Dopamine is a neurotransmitter that gives you pleasure. We all like pleasure, so this is another reason it may be difficult to cut out your caffeine—you find yourself missing that rush of pleasure you typically get with your morning cup of coffee.

Coffee does not give you energy but actually drains your body's energy stores in a desperate attempt to get the poisons out of your body. What caffeine does is block certain receptors in the brain and certain chemicals from being absorbed into your brain that would normally make you feel tired. These poisons come from—you guessed it—coffee.

But that's bad because your body winds up functioning at a higher level when what it needs to do is rest. Resting is when healing occurs. So, if you prevent yourself from resting, you're not giving your body a chance to heal, and the damage that you're doing to yourself now becomes more and more cumulative, and at some point, becomes irreversible.

Coffee robs your body of energy. Caffeine in coffee also robs your body of its ability to rest. The body overrides the caffeine and forces you to get tired. So what do you do? You drink more coffee! That's why if one cup of coffee used to "do the trick," you now have to drink two or three cups of coffee to keep you awake. Eventually, you drink so much caffeine that you're able to drink caffeine and go right to bed because your body is trying to override the caffeine every way it can—another stress on the nervous system and in our lives, which we don't need!

Coffee's high in caffeine. That's why we drink it. We like it. Coffee's also high in a lot of other chemicals. And coffee is also an acid. It stains your teeth. Stains your clothes. Stains your rug. It's a *very strong* acid, and we've already discussed the dangers of putting acids in your body.

## *The Little Extras You Get with Coffee*

Let's assume that you were going to drink a cup of regular coffee. The kind you make at home, not the fancy kind that you spend too much money for at the trendy place where they read poetry, sell CDs, and provide an office for people who don't have one of their own.

Before you make that cup of coffee, consider this: there's only one other product on the market today that has more synthetic pesticides than coffee. And that's tobacco. Brad Rodu, in his article "Carcinogens in Coffee and Smokeless Tobacco: Truths & Half-Truths," notes:

> *In a single cup of coffee, the natural chemicals that are known rodent carcinogens are about equal in weight to a year's worth of synthetic pesticide residues that are rodent carcinogens, even though only 3% of the natural chemicals in roasted coffee have been adequately tested for carcinogenicity.*

So, in one cup of coffee you'll be exposed to more synthetic pesticides than you would if you ate nonorganic fruits and vegetables for an entire year! Because you know I like to repeat myself for effect, here I go. If we went to a grocery store, a plain old grocery store, a can of coffee is likely to have more synthetic pesticides than all the fruits and vegetables in the whole store. Wow! That's bad stuff. Think about it.

Have you ever heard someone say, "I can't go to the bathroom until I've had my morning coffee?" Did you ever wonder about that? Coffee contains so many poisons that the body almost immediately responds to it by doing everything in its power to rid itself of the offending toxin. Therefore, the trip to the bathroom. And people think they are doing something great for their body by drinking coffee! That coffee actually just stimulated your bowels to cleanse themselves of the poisons you just poured into your body.

Coffee is also a diuretic—it makes you pee. It dehydrates you. And again, it's an acid, which robs your body of calcium.

Whenever you put something that's not good for you into your body, your body does one of two things:

- Stores it
- Passes it out

You drink coffee, what happens? One cup of coffee, you start to sweat a little bit. You probably need to go tinkle. After two cups of coffee, you're grabbing a book and running to the bathroom. Why? We've covered this before—drinking coffee opens up every route of detoxification, so things come out of your body. Coffee is an irritating acid that makes your bowels work in emergency overtime mode.

So coffee is not the drink of choice.

### The Decaf Myth

You say to me, "Dr. Joe, I'm smarter than you; I don't drink regular coffee, I drink decaf." DECAF! AUUGGHH!

What does decaffeinated coffee actually mean? Any idea? *Some* of the caffeine—operative word being *some*—has been removed. Decaffeinated actually means *less* caffeine than the straight stuff. It doesn't mean that there's *no* caffeine in it. If you took all the caffeine out, the coffee would be almost flavorless. Most people have no idea what decaffeinated coffee actually is.

And most people have no idea that the process to decaffeinate coffee can involve turpentine and formaldehyde. Yup, you got it. The stuff used to embalm people. I'm repeating for emphasis here: One of the ways we decaffeinate coffee is with turpentine and formaldehydes.

The only time I want formaldehyde in my body is when I'm dead. Wait, no, not even then.

# The Price of Addiction

I knew a woman who developed cysts in her breasts. Her doctor advised her to stop drinking coffee, so of course, she 100 percent complied—as all patients of all health professionals do. Right? Riiiiight.

No, since she knew best, this woman "just" drank decaf. And as we now know, we really should put quotes around "decaf" coffee, because there is no such animal. She said the lumps grew much smaller on the decaf. (And this is great news?) But whenever she got into the regular coffee, they would get bigger and harder again.

Call me crazy, but I call her crazy. And this woman also watched her beloved husband, a two-liter-a-day diet cola addict, lose a kidney, endure years of dialysis, and finally succumb to nephritis, an inflammation of the kidneys. Risk factors for nephritis, a potentially fatal disease? Consumption of coffee and artificial sweeteners. Oh yeah, and smoking.

I know this woman smoked, so there's a good probability that her husband did as well. At the very least, he was exposed to her secondhand smoke. Since she was a coffee addict, I would bet money that he was at least a habitual coffee ingester, in addition to the diet cola. The poor guy never stood a chance.

I had another patient who told me he drank 48 cups of coffee a day—every day. I said, "You have to be dead from that."

"Captain Insano," I christened him in my mind. I assume he was telling me the truth, but I don't know how he could be alive while drinking that much coffee, because his body would be so depleted.

I think he might have been fibbing to me about the number of cups. But, still, I could tell he drank a lot of coffee. His muscles were like rocks. I mean, I'd go to adjust him, and nothing would move. Eventually I said to him, "You gotta give up the coffee because I can't help you."

He stopped coming to see me. He couldn't give up his coffee. He was that much of an addict.

So let's assume we go to one of these fancy-schmancy coffeehouses and we spend $6 for a cup of coffee. Why do you think it tastes so good? What makes it different? It has a lot more caffeine in it. The fancy-schmancy coffeehouses have more caffeine in their coffee than the coffee you would brew at home—and that's why it tastes better (that's also why it's more addicting, by the way).

So if you went to one of those fancy-schmancy coffeehouses and got a decaffeinated cup of coffee, it would most likely have more caffeine than a regular cup of coffee that you brewed at home. Wow! That's why it tastes so good. It's the caffeine.

My decaf-drinking patients say, "Well, there's not much caffeine left in my coffee. It can't be THAT bad." Hmmm. Well, the fact remains that the stuff that IS left can cause cancer. Now, I don't know about you, but I personally don't know how much cancer is safe. And I'm a doctor.

A little cancer? I just want a little cancer, please. Thank you. I don't want a lot, because that'll kill me. I just want a little cancer. That mentality is dangerous, indeed.

## Dr. Joe's Brown Belt Suggestions to Cut Coffee Consumption

Coffee. Not the drink of choice. But I know some of you are addicted to coffee because numerous studies have proven that coffee *is* addicting. It used to take one cup of coffee to get you high, but then it took two, and then three, and then five. You may know someone, perhaps yourself, who drinks a pot of coffee a day, maybe even two pots of coffee a day.

Because I know coffee is such a huge part of many people's lives, I want to give you some in-depth brown belt suggestions for beating the coffee habit. I know coffee addiction is very real. And very dangerous.

If you're addicted to coffee, I don't want you to just stop cold turkey, because you're going to get what? Headaches. What I need to do is wean you off. Okay?

So get a cup of coffee and put it in front of you tomorrow at the time you normally drink coffee. I want you to have one tablespoon of coffee an hour. No cream, no sugar, okay? This is not for pleasure. This is medicinal.

One tablespoon of coffee an hour is going to give you just enough to get to the next hour, and then the next hour, and the next hour. What'll happen is after a few hours, you'll start to feel good. You won't get the headache. You'll think, "Hey, I forgot my coffee for that hour." Good. It'll take about three or four days if you're really a hard-core coffee addict to get off your coffee. Not a bad gig.

You really can get off the coffee wagon, so to speak. So that's a great way to wean yourself off.

In the process, you have to drink a lot of water because the water is going to hydrate your body and make you feel good and give you a ton of energy.

Next time you're tired, instead of reaching for coffee or a stimulant or chocolates, I want you to just have a couple of glasses of water. You'll be amazed at how much better you feel. Remember, coffee doesn't equal energy; it only keeps you from feeling tired.

Now don't whine at me, "Well, Dr. Joe, that's all well and good about getting off the caffeine addiction's headaches, but what about constipation?"

Well, if you're drinking all the water and eating all the fruits and veggies that you're supposed to be, that shouldn't be a problem. But if you still have problems from time to time, or during your transition from coffee addict to victor, you may want to look into some of the herbal remedies sold in health food stores. I created a supplement called Dr. Joe's Intestinal Cleanser to help get your bowels back on track. More information on this and all of my supplements can be found at drjoeesposito.com. You can also toss a heapin' helpin' of ground chia and/or flaxseeds into your smoothie with Dr. Joe's Essential Source and Dr. Joe's Super Greens. I promise that'll have your train schedule running on time and you won't need any assistance from anything in a bottle.

To progressively "step down" from coffee, drink mate (pronounced mah-tay) tea. To progress downward in caffeine levels, consider working yourself through these beverages with decreasing levels of caffeine:

- Coffee
- Mate tea
- Black tea
- Green tea
- White tea

## Tea Talk

Before we leave tea, I'd like to say a word about "decaffeinated" tea. This sounds way healthier than regular tea, and especially better than coffee, right? Not so fast. There are three ways to remove caffeine. The first two sound pretty dastardly to me. They call them "organic" chemical solvents, but that is an oxymoron if I ever saw one.

Yes, sir, as far as chemistry 101 is concerned, there are *two* kinds of compounds—organic and inorganic, so they technically qualify as organic. But for someone who strives to consume organic food, they are definitely not on the Nice List. The first is methylene chloride, and the second is ethyl acetate. You might as well shake one of those pastel colored packets into your cup if you're gonna put up with that!

The third method makes me want to start singing "Edelweiss." It's the Swiss method. And those people know from clean and pure. They use *water* to extract the caffeine. Sounds a little bit better, doesn't it? But you're going to have to make like Sherlock Holmes and inspect the packaging to discover which method has been used for the tea you want to buy. You may even have to do some Googling, but there is a huge difference in the decaf process, and I want you to be knowledgeable and careful about what you're drinking.

I'd also like to put in a plug for herbal teas. We live in a wonderful world today. When I was a kid, the grocery store only carried plain old regular black tea. You had two choices: drink it, or don't. Today, any chain market will have plenty of wonderful choices of refreshing teas, comprised of all sorts of delicious things that are not camellia sinesis, which used to be the only game in town.

And if you take yourself to one of our healthier-choice, more-evolved chains, there are more truly caffeine-free choices than all the tea in China. As any addict of any stripe knows, you often need to replace an addiction with something else. Tea is a really easy substitution for coffee. Most of the big brands work hard to put these teas in boxes covered with beautiful art. Think of the tea aisle as your candy store!

Have fun and try all different kinds until you settle on some favorites. And raise a cup to me (with your pinky out, of course) and drink to your health!

Remember: if something says "caffeine-free," it never had caffeine to begin with. If something says "decaffeinated," it had caffeine and some of it was taken out, but there's still some caffeine left. Most people never think that one through thoroughly.

## Cool, Clear Water

And here's one more tip.

Just drink water.

Drink it, as much as you can, within reason. You'll be fascinated how much better you feel if you just drink water—even if you do nothing else I'm recommending. If you take nothing else from this book today, I want you to increase your water intake.

Save yourself the six bucks from your fancy-schmancy coffee and have some water. Your body will thank you for giving it a much-needed rest. You're dealing with enough toxins and stressors outside your body. If you want to keep it in its best working condition for the longest possible duration, give it a rest from toxins and stressors inside it.

# Sodas

Sodas can contain 9 to 12 teaspoons of sugar per can. In addition, colas contain a large amount of phosphoric acid—if you pour a can of cola on your car, you can actually watch it eat the paint off of your car! The "bubbly water" in soda is also an acid. If you've ever spilled something on your shirt or tie, and you've used club soda to get rid of the stain, you've seen an acid in action. So if you put soda in your body, your body has to neutralize that acid.

Again, your body has to work hard and use its valuable sources of calcium and other minerals to neutralize these acids.

Not only does soda contain lots of sugars and acids, but the very package it's delivered in can also be harmful! Soda cans are often lined with Bisphenol A, better known as BPA, which has been linked to cancer, fertility problems, and a whole host of other health issues. Soda may appear to temporarily quench your thirst, but it actually is a diuretic and will drain your body of vital fluids and nutrients.

And there are even more problems with soda, as noted by Beth Levine in the following article "Preventing Cancer and Diabetes by Not Drinking Sodas" (originally published on www.jonbarron.org; copyright © 1999-2015 Baseline of Health® Foundation; used by permission of the Baseline of Health® Foundation; all rights reserved worldwide).

*No one thinks of sugary soda as a healthy choice for a beverage. But most drinkers will defend their habit by saying it isn't dangerous, and a few glasses a day isn't going to do any harm. Unfortunately for them, soda drinkers may be very wrong.*

*A new study has found that consuming soda every day may be connected to the development of kidney disease. The research, which took place at Osaka University in Japan, determined that adults who drink more than two sodas daily face a greater chance of showing early signs of kidney damage.*

*The subjects were more than 12,000 adults employed by the university. During their annual physical exam at the health center, the participants answered questions about their eating habits including the frequency of their soda consumption. Additionally, a urine sample was taken and analyzed for the presence of protein. Protein in the urine is one of the initial signs of kidney damage, which is often still reversible at that point. There was a follow-up period of three years from the start of the study.*

*Over the course of that time, almost 11 percent of the volunteers who reported drinking a minimum of two sodas containing sugar every day were found to have protein in their urine. That is an increase over the approximately nine percent with protein in their urine who said they typically consumed one can per day and the 8.4 percent with protein in their urine who never drank soda.*

*These differences may not seem enormous, but when the population sampled includes 12,000 individuals, that means several hundred more people were then suffering from an early symptom of kidney damage that can be associated with steady soft drink consumption. And protein in the urine may indicate other diseases on the horizon as well as potentially serious kidney problems.*

*A 2012 study at the Mario Negri Institute for Pharmacological*

*Research in Bergamo, Italy found that even a minuscule amount of protein in the urine might be linked with an increased risk of cardiovascular disease in those with Type 2 diabetes.*

*While the current research was not designed to prove a cause-and-effect relationship between drinking soda and kidney disease, the evidence is mounting from other sources that sugar may be a key factor in damage to this organ.*

*A recent study conducted at Case Western Reserve University in Cleveland, Ohio, discovered that even moderate amounts of fructose can alter the kidneys' ability to properly regulate salt balance. Maintaining the correct levels of sodium and water in the body is an important function of the kidneys. Using rats as their study subjects, the scientists found that the changes taking place caused the cells of the kidneys to reabsorb a greater quantity of salt.*

*This may be why soda—which often contains substantial quantities of high fructose corn syrup—has been implicated in the development of not only kidney problems, but also diabetes, high blood pressure, and obesity. This is bad news for people who are working on preventing diabetes.*

*In fact, in 2010, researchers at the University of Southern California's Keck School of Medicine in Los Angeles analyzed samples from numerous soft drinks and discovered that many contain even more fructose than their labels indicated. And soft drink consumption is higher than ever, with a 2011 survey showing that carbonated soft drinks are the most commonly consumed beverages in the United States (although sales have ebbed in the years since).*

*Not to mention the fact that all those who are trying to avoid the sugar and reaching for diet sodas instead are no better off. These artificially sweetened drinks have been linked to certain forms of cancer, cardiovascular disease, osteoporosis, osteoarthritis, and more. If preventing cancer is important to you, then you should try to stay away from diet sodas.*

Hey, that's not Dr. Joe talking, it's the scientists! Told you I'm not wrong! After looking at the research, Levine notes:

*Maybe an occasional glass of soda won't hurt, but this is one habit with little redeeming value and plenty of potential for harm. Preventing diabetes and preventing cancer will be more difficult if you drink sodas on a regular basis. Switching to water will help properly hydrate your body, keeping the gastrointestinal tract and kidneys functioning optimally.*

## Dr. Joe's Brown Belt Suggestions to Cut Soda Consumption

If you have to drink soda, there are sodas made with stevia or—even better—you can make your own with one of the latest home soda-maker machines. Stevia and lemon juice can make an amazing lemon soda, or you can use other frozen concentrated organic juices. True, pure juice has an overly high sugar content, but it is better than the high fructose corn syrup in most commercial sodas today.

To make your own soda:

- Pour 8 ounces of chilled, salt-free seltzer into a glass.
- Add 2 tablespoons of frozen juice concentrate (orange, grape, lemon, grapefruit, apple, etc.).
- Stir well and enjoy!

Make sure the seltzer bottle is glass because the acid in the seltzer could dissolve plastic, and plastic can act as an endocrine disruptor.

## Hold the Salt and Pass the Seltzer

A special note about the differences between club soda and seltzer.

Club soda contains salts. Seltzer does not. The salts add a different flavor, especially when mixed with alcohol, which you're not supposed to be drinking anyway! If I had to pick one, I'd pick seltzer.

When you eat salt, it causes your salivary glands to release saliva. Saliva contains amylase, which breaks down sugars. So, when you add something with a little salt to something sweet, it actually tastes sweeter. What's bad is that the salt they use in club soda is not a good salt. The salts used are often heated at over 1,200 degrees. At that temperature, vital nutrients and minerals are often destroyed, making it a toxic chemical.

If you're going to use salt, it needs to be air- or sun-dried sea salt. A good example would be Celtic sea salt, pink salts, or Himalayan sea salt. A good way to tell if you have a good salt is that it is not pure white. It can be pink, grey, black, but not pure white. Pure white means it has been processed and is no longer healthy. In fact, I do recommend you eat at least a quarter teaspoon of air-dried sea salt every day. It has over 70 minerals in it and is actually good for you.

# Artificial Sweeteners

Okay, all of you diet soda drinkers, get ready to hate my guts! I'm going to talk about a subject that fosters intense controversy and strongly entrenched beliefs on both sides. In the long run, however, you are going to thank me for pouring this bucket of cold water on your good feelings about diet drinks—and other food and drinks that contain artificial sweeteners.

If you decide to rid your diet of just one of the Seven Deadly Sins—alcohol, meat, sugar, dairy, coffee, soda, and artificial sweeteners—I want you to make artificial sweeteners the number one thing to go.

## Aspartame

We'll talk about aspartame first. Aspartame is a substance manufactured by combining the amino acids L-Phenylalanine and L-Aspartic acid with the ester of methyl alcohol, which converts into methanol, which is wood alcohol. Is it good to drink or ingest into your body? Not at all! These molecules break down into diketopiperazine, an agent that has been shown in various medical studies to cause brain tumors.

Is it good to drink or ingest methanol? No way! Methanol can cause brain damage and blindness. During Prohibition, some alcoholics drank wood alcohol and went blind. Wood alcohol is methanol. And methanol converts to formaldehyde, which converts to formic acid, which is used as an ant poison. Now repeat after me: methanol converts to formaldehyde! Formaldehyde is embalming fluid! Add in a little ant poison and you've got a great cocktail!

And there's more. Aspartame can lower your serotonin levels. Serotonin is the magical component that keeps you calm and focused, remember?

Aspartame can get into the brain, but it has a tough time getting out of the brain. Some studies now indicate that if you build up these chemicals, it can cause brain cancer. Aspartame can create astrocytomas in your body, which grow up to become gliomas. Gliomas, good people, are brain cancer.

When you put aspartame in your body, it converts to three components—aspartic acid, phenylalanine, and methyl esters. Aspartic acid in the body is known as an excitotoxin; it causes the brain to fire faster than it is supposed to and can actually burn out and kill brain cells. You need some aspartic acid in your brain for it to function normally. But when you drink isolated and concentrated forms of aspartic acid (like from artificial sweeteners), it can cause damage. A little bit found in proteins in natural form, that's okay. Concentrated and isolated? Not so much and not so good.

Yet people go on and on, consuming this poison by the gallon every single day. I don't get it. Number one side effect of aspartame? Headaches. Drinks with artificial sweeteners in them—not at all the drink of choice. Worst. Drink. Ever.

## Sucralose

Now, the yellow packet you see on tables in restaurants, sucralose, is actually chlorinated hydrocarbon. Sweetener companies take sugar through a five-step process. They subtract an OH group and basically add chlorine to it. So what does that mean to us English-speaking folks?

When a chlorinated hydrocarbon gets into your body, it stimulates your estrogen receptor sites. Estrogen receptor sites cause your body to produce estrogen. Now, why is that bad? Estrogen is a growth hormone.

If you're reading this book, you are most likely grown up. But your growth hormones are being overstimulated as you continue to guzzle down diet soda after diet soda. If you're not growing bigger and stronger, then that means you're growing wider and fatter.

Plus, estrogen also stimulates cell growth, and too much estrogen can cause abnormal cell growth. What happens if we have too much abnormal cell growth? We call that cancer. Wow. Thanks, sweetener companies.

Now men are under the mistaken impression that anything related to estrogen applies only to their mothers, wives, sisters, or girlfriends. Not so fast, my friend.

Guys, as we get older we start to lose some of our abilities, if you know what I mean. One of the things we lose is testosterone. Our testosterone levels start to drop as we move into our 20s and 30s and really begin to plummet in our 40s and 50s. Hence, the multiple TV commercials you are seeing for "Low T" and the little blue pill.

If men use artificial sweeteners, that stimulates their estrogen receptor sites to produce more estrogen, just like the gals. The estrogen counteracts the testosterone they have, so now men need those little blue pills because the equipment "just don't work like it used to." As we get older, male and female testosterone levels are naturally going to drop. But we don't want to add to that by consuming artificial sweeteners.

And just so I'm an equal opportunity offender, women, listen up. Too much estrogen is wreaking havoc on the average American woman's life, too. Estrogen can stimulate or worsen certain types of breast cancer. You really want to drink something that is going to crank up your body to produce more estrogen so that your chances of getting cancer are even higher? In original studies, aspartame was shown to have caused more mammary tumors than brain tumors.

Great. Not to mention that these same sweeteners actually make it harder to lose weight? Wake up, America! Diet sodas WILL MAKE YOU FEEL HUNGRY! Guess what most people do when they feel hungry? They eat. Kind of defeats the whole purpose, doesn't it? Studies have shown that diet soda drinkers are actually more overweight than regular soda drinkers. Heck, just put yourself in the non-soda-drinker category, and maybe you can save a couple of hours a week on the elliptical.

## Repeating Again

OK, now. This is the section where I repeat myself a lot. A whole lot. Keep reading anyway.

Aspartame can actually cause you to gain weight because it is stored in fat cells, especially in the hips and buttocks. Read that sentence again.

Because you want to lose some weight, you are consuming an artificial sweetener that is scientifically known to cause you to gain weight. Now, I'm no rocket scientist, but I think you might want to review your weight loss plan.

I feel like I'm taking crazy pills. Cuckoo McNutt Bird crazy. (That's one of my "Dr. Joe-isms.") I can't seem to convince people how horrible these drinks are for them.

Aspartame will convert to methanol, a form of alcohol known to cause vision problems and blindness. I believe you might want to review your weight loss plan when one of the foundations of the plan is an artificially sweetened beverage that is known to:

- Make you hungry
- Make you gain weight
- Cause vision problems and blindness

The only thing I can figure out is that folks keep drinking these drinks because eventually they will not be able to see how obese they've grown. Is that the plan?

Aspartame is incredibly addicting, and methanol is being classified as a narcotic. This affects the dopamine system of your brain, creating and causing the addiction.

Remember when artificial sweeteners first became popular? Those little pink packets used to—as God is my witness—actually say on them that studies have shown that this product can cause cancer!

Now, this was written in pink ink on pink paper, which I always found interesting. Nice and difficult for the user to read! Gotta love those sweetener manufacturers! And which gender is their top consumer? Yep. Pink is for girls. They know their market.

Of course, the next sweetener maker to come along knew pink was already taken, so they went for blue. And then there's the yellow packets; I guess to keep up with the pastel theme.

Now if a product says on its own label that it causes cancer, call me crazy, but I personally would believe it. They're not making that up! And you know they didn't *want* to put it on there. It has since been taken off the label, but it's still the same product, with the same outcomes.

As if the SAD American diet weren't bad enough, there is another reality in our great nation that money talks, and facts walk. So just because artificial sweetener manufacturers were allowed to remove their cautionary tale from that packet, doesn't mean the danger disappeared. Many European countries are way ahead of us in banning toxic food ingredients. Yep, the standard American diet really does make me SAD.

A warning that hasn't been removed from the packages of artificial sweeteners deals with phenylalanine, another amino acid, that is processed in your body. If you can't process this amino acid properly, it can cause kidney damage. Something called phenylketonuria, which can be deadly. So artificial sweeteners carry warnings something like this: "Aspartame must not be used by people with the metabolic genetic disorder Phenylketonuria (PKU)."

Most newborn babies in the U.S. are screened for PKU upon birth. Some of the symptoms of this disease can present themselves as albinism, seizures, and/or complete or partial absence of pigment in the skin, hair or eyes. People who have this condition are generally advised to avoid foods high in phenylalanine such as meat, chicken, fish, eggs, nuts, cheese, legumes and dairy products.

Sounds vaguely like the Seven Deadly Sins, doesn't it?

Let me say it one more time: Artificial sweeteners are not good for you. In fact, they're rather dangerous. Study after study has been performed with the same outcomes. And yet, people continue in this blind walk down this VERY dangerous road.

# Boosting Productivity

Corporations hire me to give wellness workshops because they want to increase the productivity of their employees. I get to travel all over the world. It's a lot of fun. And I get paid for it.

When I'm finished presenting my material, inevitably, the human resources director comes up to me and says, "We need to get that stuff, artificial sweeteners, sugar, coffee—you know, the Seven Deadly Sins—out of our break room."

Why do they say this to me? If a big company can increase productivity by just 5 percent, how much money would that equate to? These companies are ready to get rid of these substances because they know their employees will be more productive.

What if we increased your productivity 5 percent? What would that mean to you? Quality of life, quantity of life, ability to earn, ability to be a good spouse, family member, church member, whatever your goals are. So stay away from the artificial sweeteners—and the other six deadly sins too!

## *Take the Aspartame Challenge*

In reality, this should be called the "Any Artificial Sweetener Challenge." It's really simple.

- Cut out all artificial sweeteners for 100 days.
- See how you feel.
- In 100 days, start consuming artificial sweeteners again.
- See how you feel.

I'm not here to argue with you, but what I'm telling you is what I've learned from the research and from well over 30 years of practice. I've never seen anyone NOT do better when they gave up artificial sweeteners.

If I'm wrong (and I'm not), then so what? You changed your habits for a little more than three months—that's all. But if I'm right (and I am), then we just saved you a lot of needless suffering.

So, pick your battles. Diet soda's not the drink of choice. For anyone. I can't make it any plainer than that. At some point, you have to look at the science and make an educated decision about your health and your life.

I told you that you would probably hate me after this section. In the long run, however, you are going to thank me.

Dr. Joseph Mercola wrote a great article called "Sugar Substitutes— What's Safe and What's Not" that sums up the disadvantages of all types of sweeteners. His article is a great summation of the many negative results I've outlined here. Look this article up on the Internet. You may be shocked by what you read.

### Dr. Joe's Brown Belt Suggestions to Cut Artificial Sweetener Consumption

You may not want to go off of sweeteners "cold turkey" because that could cause you to experience headaches and other symptoms, similar to caffeine withdrawal. I suggest that you discuss your decision with your integrative medical doctor or your chiropractor. They will have some suggestions to help you through this process.

There is something called "energy medicine." Energy medicine involves a systematic process called "tapping," which is used on people who have addictions. "Turbo tapping" can help the body physiologically break addictive cravings. Not everyone embraces this treatment, but if you are struggling, you might want to check into it. Any practitioner who works with EFT (Emotional Freedom Techniques) will be familiar with tapping. Personally, I've seen amazing results with this technique and highly recommend it. Look it up online, watch some of the videos and give it a try!

If you don't believe anything I've said in this section, I recommend that you take this 100-day test if you are a heavy artificial sweetener user and you are having symptoms that you can't seem to explain.

# Stop Sinning to Live Longer, Feel Better

In my office, I have a list of seven foods you should never eat. As you know by now, I call them the "Seven Deadly Sins." You've been reading all about these for the last several pages, but just in case you have forgotten, I'll remind you that dairy products are not the food of choice. Nor is alcohol, meat, sugar, coffee, soda, or artificial sweeteners. Those are not the foods of choice, and yet they're what most people eat. Even though they probably know that most of these things are not good for them.

I believe we are designed to live 120 years, and I see no reason why we shouldn't. Except that we keep committing the Seven Deadly Sins every day instead of nourishing our body. As a child you have good stores of nutrients; in fact, you start out with everything you need to reach 120 years of age.

But we short-circuit ourselves because we are not informed about the Seven Deadly Sins, and we wind up taking nutrients away from our body without knowing it. Or worse, we have the knowledge and do nothing about it.

Don't be one of the sheep, blindly following others into the ditch. You deserve better. Avoiding the Seven Deadly Sins is the best place to start. Then you'll be ready to go even further on the road toward good health—a road that we will explore in the next chapters.

CHAPTER

# More Nutrition Secrets from Dr. Joe

As I said in the previous chapter, nutrition is one of the key building blocks of a healthy life. And healthy eating habits are key to getting the right nutrition. We talked a lot about the Seven Deadly Sins in the past chapter, but there is more to nutrition and healthy eating than just avoiding bad stuff. You have to figure out the best ways to deliver the good stuff to your body; that is what will help you protect your immune system and ensure good digestion.

## The Dangers of Cooking Your Food

If you cook your foods, they will put stress on your immune system. Once a food, even a healthy food, is heated above 110 degrees Fahrenheit, it begins to lose its nutrients and put stress on your immune system.

For example, if you eat a raw vegetable, such as a carrot, or a raw fruit, there is almost no increase in your white blood cell count. White blood cells are the part of the immune system that will attack "bad" invaders in the system. When you eat the same amount of cooked carrots, the white blood cell count increases dramatically, indicating that the immune system is attacking the cooked food.

Many folks are not willing to convert to an all-raw fruit and vegetable diet, but the more cooked food we eat, the more we stress the immune system.

If we cook meat, we destroy a lot of vitamins, minerals, and nutrients. That's why if you fed cooked meat to a carnivore, it would get sick and eventually die. Do an Internet search on Dr. Francis Pottenger's cat studies. He fed one group of cats primarily raw meat and one group of cats a diet that included cooked meat.

Dr. Pottenger found that after the third generation, most of the cats that ate the cooked meat were sterile or they had high numbers of stillborn births and small litters. That group of cats in general just didn't do as well as the group who ate raw meat. Kooky old Dr. Pottenger even separated the waste products from the two groups of cats. The area that contained the waste products of the animals that ate the cooked meat never had weeds grow there. Bugs wouldn't even go there.

Pottenger's studies are just one of the reasons I think we're not designed to eat cooked meat. Now that being said, don't eat raw meat—remember our earlier discussions about parasites and other such problems?

But do think about cooking less.

The less you cook food, the better. And be especially sure to avoid those grill marks you see on hamburgers; those tempting-looking grill marks create heterocyclic amines, which are known carcinogens. In English, that means: *this can cause cancer.*

If you're a griller, you're not doing yourself any favors. As you grill, the fat of the meat drips down on the coals, and the smoke that is created contains polycyclic aromatic hydrocarbons. And guess what? They, too, are carcinogens!

More and more evidence links grilling, smoking, and frying food to cancer. In his article "Cooking Up Cancer?" Brian Palmer states:

> *A growing body of research suggests that cooking meats over a flame is linked to cancer. Combusting wood, gas, or charcoal emits chemicals known as polycyclic aromatic hydrocarbons. Exposure to these so-called PAHs is known to cause skin, liver, stomach, and several other types of cancer in lab animals. Epidemiological studies link occupational exposure to PAHs to cancer in humans. When PAHs from a flame mingle with nitrogen, say from a slab of meat, they can form nitrated PAHs, or NPAHs. NPAHs are even more carcinogenic than PAHs in laboratory experiments. The reasonable conclusion is that grilling meat may be hazardous to your health.*

Many people have never considered the fact that eating a grilled steak may supply your body with about as many carcinogens as smoking a cigarette. Next time you feel like firing up the grill for a Fourth of July picnic, consider this: the grill marks on your steak, chicken, and even vegetables contain carcinogens.

### Don't Touch That Dial!

Okay, here is Dr. Joe shouting at you now:

# NEVER, UNDER ANY CIRCUMSTANCES, MICROWAVE ANYTHING!

To explain why, I'm going to refer to Dr. Joseph Mercola, particularly an article found on his website, "Why Did the Russians Ban an Appliance Found in 90% of American Homes?" Mercola does a great job of combining the scientific research citations with an easy-to-understand writing style.

Here are two highlights from just one of his articles on microwave use:

*Some studies suggest microwaving your food can potentially expose you to carcinogenic toxins released from plastic or paper wrappers, destruction of valuable nutrients in the food, and radiation leakage.*

*Swiss food scientist Dr. Hans Hertel found that microwaved food increased cholesterol levels, decreased both red and white blood cell counts, decreased hemoglobin, and produced radiolytic compounds.*

Microwaving your food alters the protein in it, and altered protein in the body can cause all types of damage, including the "C" word. There is SO much research out there that you've already heard, I don't need to beat this one to death.

If you're like me, you'll find that the microwave is great for only two things:

1. Zapping your dishwashing cloths to kill germs. At the end of every day, put your non-metal dishwashing sponge in the microwave for two minutes and walk away. Since most microwaves leak radiation, I don't want you getting zapped!

2. Serving as an extra cabinet in your kitchen where you can store your pots and pans!

## *Dr. Joe's Brown Belt Suggestions for Healthier Cooking*

If you are dead set on eating meat, marinate it in lemon juice or raw, organic apple cider vinegar with rosemary to help reduce the levels of heterocyclic amines.

Raw vegetables are best, but if you must cook, steaming is the best way to prepare them so that they don't lose their nutritional value. After that (going from best to worst), the cooking methods that will be most beneficial are:

- Baked
- Quickly fried
- Broiled
- Grilled (I bet you thought grilled vegetables were one of the healthiest things you could eat!)

And no matter what method you use, the less you cook your vegetables, the better off you'll be.

If you're going to fry, make sure you use the proper oils. Remember that canola, corn, soy and cottonseed oils usually contain GMOs, which you want to avoid at all costs. And you should NEVER use hydrogenated oils.

# Juicing

People talk about juicing all the time, and juicing can be a really good thing—depending on *what* you're juicing. Juicing vegetables is better for you than juicing fruit. If you juice fruits, you're going to get a lot of fructose, and there's more and more evidence coming out that too much fructose is extremely dangerous.

# Smoke Points

Different oils have different smoke points, which means they will start smoking at different temperatures. Once oil starts to smoke, it becomes toxic. Heating oil produces free fatty acid, and as heating time increases, more free fatty acids are produced, thereby decreasing the smoke point.

This is one reason not to use the same oil to deep-fry more than twice. Intermittent frying has a markedly greater effect on oil deterioration than continuous frying.

The best oils to cook with are the ones that have the highest smoke points. Those are:

- Rice bran oil: 490°F
- Mustard oil: 489°F
- Peanut oil: 450°F
- Sesame oil: (refined) 450°F
- Hazelnut oil: 430°F
- Grapeseed oil: 420°F
- Palm oil (refined): 420°F
- Macadamia oil: 410°F
- Walnut oil: 400°F
- Olive oil: 375°F
- Coconut oil (virgin): 350°F
- Hemp oil: 330°F
- Unrefined sesame oil: 320°F
- Safflower oil (virgin): 225°F
- Sunflower oil (virgin): 225°F
- Flaxseed oil: 225°F

# Sugar and Uric Acid

Your body can process about 20 to 25 grams of fructose a day. That's about three to four pieces of fruit along with other sources of fructose most people get in their diet. Anything beyond that can cause the liver to produce something called uric acid, which can really hurt you when it gets into your joints.

This condition has been around ever since man has been able to overeat. It's one of the reasons the ancient Romans set up spas around mineral springs all over their empire. Some of the U.S. Founding Fathers suffered from this condition. It's called gout. And it ain't just for fat old men, let me tell you! I see gout in a lot of my patients who don't even consider themselves middle-aged!

Uric acid can create crystals in all your joints. As a chiropractor, I see people with joint pain every day all day long. And even though I can do amazing chiropractic work to relieve joint pain, I need patients to help me, too. If they're putting a lot of fructose into the body, that fructose is going to get into their joints, cause inflammation, and irritate the joints.

If that's not bad enough, uric acid also prevents the body from producing enough nitric oxide, which is a vasodilator—that means it opens up your blood vessels. Nitric oxide is vital for heart, brain, and muscle function—and most importantly for reproductive function, another very important part of your life! Both men and women need nitric oxide to create fireworks; if you don't have enough nitric oxide, the blood vessels can't open up enough to create the proper engorging reactions.

Many times, people come to me and say, "Doc, I'm having trouble in the bedroom," and it turns out they're not producing enough nitric oxide. This applies to both men and women.

## Juicing Fruit

So I don't recommend juicing fruit because fruit juices contains more fructose than your body can process properly. Now, if you eat a piece of fruit, you will also be getting the fiber that's in the fruit, and the fiber's going to slowly push the sugar through the colon and give you a slow release of the sugar. If you drink the pure juice—BANG!—you get this big rush and a big blood sugar spike. So save your juicing for vegetables. And don't eat more than three or four pieces of whole fruit a day, max.

Obviously, I think fruit juice is a bad idea. And commercial juices are even worse than making your own because most commercial juices have high fructose corn syrup and chemicals added to them in addition to being heated and pasteurized, which destroys many nutrients. If the juice you buy has a "best if used by" date more than 60 days in the future, you know it's been loaded with chemicals to preserve it.

Pure, fresh, unpasteurized fruit juice does go bad—and that's good! There's a good rule about eating: if the food doesn't go bad, don't eat it!

If you're a parent and you think you're doing something good for your kids by giving them fruit juices, think again. Worse than fruit juice is something that says "made with fruit juice," because "made with fruit juice" is pretty much sugar water and chemicals. There is very little fruit juice in there, as low as 10 percent in most. If 100 percent fruit juice isn't good, 10 percent fruit juice is even worse.

Even worse is something called a "fruit drink." That usually means a beverage that is almost pure sugar with some food coloring, and *maybe* a little bit of fruit, but just maybe.

## Juicing Vegetables

I think it's an excellent idea to juice vegetables. Vegetable cells have a wall around them called cellulose, which requires an enzyme called cellulase to break down. We humans don't produce a lot of cellulase, so we can get the nutrients out of vegetables by chewing, which mechanically opens the cells.

Alternatively, we can heat vegetables, allowing the water inside the cell to get hot and expand, but this destroys some of the nutrients. Or we can juice vegetables, which is probably the "cellulasebuster" that gives you the biggest bang for your buck.

When you juice the vegetables, you've got to drink them relatively quickly because they oxidize, or break down. If you want to add something sweet to vegetable juice, maybe add a piece of fruit. Remember, only one piece of fruit.

Granny Smith apples are your best bet; they don't spike the blood sugar as much as other fruits because they have a lower fructose content than other fruit. If you use a regular apple or an orange, that's okay, but remember that you should have no more than three or four pieces of fruit per day—less if you're getting sugars from other sources.

Instead of fruit, you can add some carrots to your concoction. But carrots are high in sugar as well, so be careful. No more than three to four medium-sized carrots a day.

Green leafy vegetables such as kale, chard, spinach, and field greens are best for juicing. You can do celery, but please, organic only.

# Dr. Joe's Essential Source Supplement

If you are challenged by not always being able to eat right, I recommend using my product Essential Source. You can get similar nutrients in one serving of Essential Source that you would get from about 10 servings of raw fruits and vegetables. Then we add prebiotics, probiotics, digestives enzymes, and a full spectrum of multivitamins. This delicious organic vegetarian powder contains:

- Fruit and vegetable complexes
- Probiotics
- Rich marine complex to aid thyroid regulation
- Complete full spectrum multivitamins (no iron)

The no-iron component of my supplement is important because many men have too much iron in their blood, which can oxidize—essentially rust—in the blood vessels, increasing the risk of heart disease. If you have too much iron in your blood, one option is to cut iron-rich foods and supplements from your diet. Another option is to simply donate blood!

Dr. Joe's Essential Source is a nutritional supplement that is among the leaders of red and green nutritional drinks in the nutraceutical industry. The proof is in the formulation, raw materials, and nutritional facts. Dr. Joe's Essential Source will make it easier for you to combine your fruit and vegetable intake with a full spectrum multivitamin. There is no need to pay more for additional vitamins if you're taking Dr. Joe's Essential Source. One scoop will give you all the antioxidant/phytonutrient and full spectrum multivitamin protection most people need.

Read the supplemental fact panel on Essential Source, and you will know without a doubt that you are getting the fruits, vegetables, and vitamins you need for optimal health benefits. And there are only 35 calories per serving in an 11-gram scoop, so it's perfect to boost healthy weight loss!

Dr. Joe's Essential Source has one of the highest ratings for oxygen radical absorbance capacity (ORAC) of any formula on the market: between 10,000 and 13,000 ORAC per serving. In addition, just for good measure, we have added a rich marine complex with a perfect balance of five different deep-sea marine algae to help thyroid regulation. Sea vegetables are 50 times more potent than any land-based vegetable.

Dr. Joe's Essential Source is a delicious, all-natural, vegetarian, super-charged, physicians' grade, synergistic formulation. It is delicious, and it's convenient enough for the whole family to use. It can also act as an appetite suppressant by helping keep blood sugars balanced. This formula is stimulant-free, diabetic safe, and contains no gluten, sugars, corn, wheat, yeast, eggs, preservatives, or artificial sweeteners, colors, or flavors. Low-temperature processing is used on the product so that it retains all of the nutrients your body needs.

And because I like you, I'd probably also recommend SUPER GREENS!

Super Greens is a remarkable dietary supplement loaded with naturally occurring vitamins and minerals. It's packed with easily digestible vegan protein, provides a great source of soluble and insoluble fiber, and replenishes the missing omega-3 fatty acids so essential for good health. In addition, this formula, which I created for my own private use, energizes your metabolism, pumps your body with over 200 antioxidants, and packs every single cell in your body with some of the highest concentrations of life-enhancing phytochemicals known to man.

You can get all of the essential vitamins and minerals from raw fruits and vegetables by drinking just one serving of this product every day. My patients see amazing benefits by using this product.

# Water

I have patients who come into my office and say, "I haven't had a glass of water in years." I think to myself, "How do you survive?"

To boost your immune system and keep your body in peak condition, you need to drink at least eight glasses of pure filtered or distilled water every day. My recommendation is to start your day with 24 ounces of water; that's three—count 'em, three—eight-ounce glasses of water at the beginning of your day. Trust me—you're going to feel so much better.

Many of my patients tell me that they used to awaken with headaches. But when they start their days with three glasses of water, the headaches disappear. You do know that hangovers are caused by toxic chemicals and dehydration, right? Just a tidbit of knowledge for you to process about the power of water.

If you're a big-time coffee drinker, you will find that you don't need as much caffeine or other stimulants if you drink more water. That's because many times when you're tired and think you need caffeine, you're simply dehydrated and all you really need is water.

The pancreas needs water to produce bicarbonate, which is essentially baking soda, to neutralize the acidic food coming from your stomach and passing into your small intestine. If you're dehydrated, you don't produce enough bicarbonate, so the food stays in the stomach. If food stays there too long, it will essentially rot. It will give off gases as it rots, which can cause bloating, flatulence, and belching.

A good rule of thumb to know whether you're drinking enough water is to check and see whether your urine is clear. Vitamins, especially B vitamins, may turn your urine a bright yellow color, but if you're getting enough water, it should still be clear, have no stink, and have no particles floating in it.

If you find you often wake up during the night to go to the bathroom, you might want to limit your water intake after three in the afternoon. You don't want to interrupt your sleep pattern by drinking all of your water right before bedtime.

"We may find in the long run that tinned food is a deadlier weapon than the machine gun."
—George Orwell

## Nutrition and Your Immune System

Many things play a role in your immune system, including emotional stress and your nervous system. Diet and digestion also play a big role.

The four major immune system organs are the thymus, lymph glands, spleen, and tonsils. Let's talk about how these immune organs interact with the body. For example, if you don't have enough stomach acids, it affects the immune organs' ability to remove toxins from your body—another reason we always have to be looking at your digestive system!

When I was a kid, tonsils were removed like crazy—mine were taken out when I was a boy. Then doctors started to realize, "Maybe the tonsils aren't the problem. Maybe it's what's causing the tonsils to become infected that's the problem." By removing tonsils, we were often treating a symptom, not treating a cause. In more recent years, we've realized that the tonsils are one of the body's four major immune organs. Removing them means taking away about 25 percent of the body's ability to protect itself.

So why do the tonsils swell to begin with? It's usually due to an abnormally functioning nervous system, an abnormally functioning digestive system and/or a bad diet. You've heard this before? Amazing, isn't it?

In my practice, we recommend that patients get off the foods that weaken the immune system, especially sugars, including breads, cookies, cakes, doughnuts, pastas—any processed sugar. I've seen this happen time and time again. I take patients off their sugar and they go all winter without getting a cold. But if they do eat sugar, they're sick within a day or two. I've seen it happen with my staff, my patients, and me.

The key is keeping the immune system healthy. Here is a simple plan to keep the immune system working at its best. These steps will help flush impurities out of your body so that the immune system can work more efficiently:

- Avoid foods that weaken the immune system, such as the Seven Deadly Sins.
- Exercise regularly, even if you start out with just a few minutes a day.
- Eat at least 60 percent of your diet from a wide variety of raw fruits, vegetables, seeds, and nuts.
- Get plenty of rest, as this is when your body heals itself.

## Immune System Boosters

Certain herbs, such as garlic and echinacea, will boost the immune system. It is especially a good idea to take these during the cold and flu season. Vitamins A, D, E, and B complex, as well as zinc and selenium, also help the immune system. The best place to get these nutrients is from raw fruits and vegetables. If you do take a supplement, it is best to get these nutrients from a supplement made from whole foods as opposed to the synthetic versions.

Dr. Mercola discusses whole food supplements on his website.

*Whole food supplements are what their name suggests: Supplements made from concentrated whole foods. The vitamins found within these supplements are not isolated. They are highly complex structures that combine a variety of enzymes, coenzymes, antioxidants, trace elements, activators and many other unknown or undiscovered factors all working together synergistically, to enable this vitamin complex to do its job in your body.*

*When you separate the vitamins from its source, it can no longer work as it was meant to without the support of the rest of the complex. Taking them in their whole form from food will allow them to work within your body as they are meant to. Synthetic supplements are just that. Synthetic. They are chemicals and isolated vitamins formed into pills containing large doses of the vitamins and can have negative effects on the body.*

*Just like refined foods, these refined vitamins have been robbed of all of the extra accessory nutrients that they naturally come with as well. In turn, like refined foods, they can create numerous problems and imbalances in your body if taken at high levels for long periods of time. They can also act more like drugs in your body, forcing themselves down one pathway or another. At the very least, they won't help you as much as high quality food and food-based supplements.*

*When looking for supplements, be sure to check the ingredients. If you find the names of foods, you've found a natural supplement. If you see chemical names or find a supplement that shows 100% daily value of a vitamin, it is a synthetic supplement. While whole food supplements and nutrients come in low-dose, they are better for your body and are more powerful than synthetic supplements.*

# A Refreshing Sleep

A good rule of thumb is to sleep long enough so that you wake up refreshed. If you have trouble getting up in the morning, go to bed earlier. If you feel like you're getting enough sleep, but you're still waking up tired, you may need to look at things like emotional stress or adrenal fatigue.

The adrenal glands are little glands that sit on top of your kidneys. If you were to cut one open, you'd see three distinct layers. One layer produces adrenaline, which helps give you energy, and one layer produces prostaglandins, which are designed to mediate inflammation; that means prostaglandins, can cause a protective inflammatory reaction, which, if you injure yourself, can actually reduce inflammation. The third layer produces DHEA, which is the building block for over 50 different hormones.

One sign of adrenal fatigue, other than feeling tired, is bags under your eyes. Look in the mirror!

Also, certain areas of the body heal themselves at specific times. For example, many hormones are replenished in the body around 9–10 p.m., so if you have hormone issues, you may want to consult with your integrative medicinal doctor about your specific recommended bedtimes.

Remember my grandfather and his words of wisdom to me: "Always buy the best. It's always cheaper." This definitely applies to vitamins and supplements, like my Essential Source and Super Greens, which are discussed above.

Look, if you want to grow a tomato plant, you need the high-quality soil, the high-quality fertilizer, pure water—all the right chemicals to produce a healthy tomato. If you want to grow and maintain a healthy body, you need the right chemicals as well. If you put low-quality chemicals in your body, you can't expect to have healthy cells.

So, do the right thing. Put all of the right things into your body so you can experience extreme health!

## Nutrition and Digestion

We've spent almost two whole chapters discussing what you should (and should NOT eat), but I want to make sure you understand something. As I have stated all through this book so far, nutrition is only one part of a great health plan. I talk with people every day who take supplements and eat the proper foods, yet they still have health issues. People tell me all the time, "I'm eating good food but I don't feel good."

What I teach (and live) is not what we ingest—it's what we digest. As I stated before, we have to look at good nutrition, but we also have to look at our nervous and digestive systems. How well are they working? Flip back to chapters 2 through 4 to get more details about those systems and how to keep them healthy.

It's vital that what you put in your body gets absorbed. Your body needs vitamins, minerals, and nutrients to operate and function properly. We all know this, but why don't we pay more attention to how the process works?

Whenever you eat, one of three things happens.

1. The food gets stored.
2. The food gets utilized.
3. The food gets passed.

If your stomach isn't digesting food properly, the food can sit in there too long and rot, producing lactic acid. Many times, if you're having acid reflux, what's coming back up into your throat is not only stomach or hydrochloric acid, it's actually lactic acid. It's the rotten food.

And so this food eventually passes into your small intestine, partially digested. If you eat a lot of sugar, it can feed bacteria and yeast in your colon, which can ferment and cause gas. If you've ever done any baking, you know that you have to add yeast and sugar to the flour to make dough. Then the yeast digests the sugar and gives off gases, which makes the dough rise. This is the exact process that occurs in your digestive system. You may think the embarrassing sound of those gases escaping is the worst that can happen to you, but trust me, what's going on silently in there is much worse!

It all makes sense now, right?

## Bacteria and Yeast

In your colon, you have about 100 different types of bacteria. In simple terms, the bacteria will eat the food that has moved into the colon and spit out what it doesn't like, and you absorb those nutrients. So you need bacteria in your colon because it is a symbiotic relationship. You feed the bacteria, the bacteria feed you.

If you take antibiotics, you can kill off the "good" bacteria as well as the "bad" bacteria causing infection. So, if you take antibiotics, you should also take something called probiotics. Probiotics ARE the good bacteria. You can also take something called prebiotics, which are essentially fertilizer for the bacteria that's already there, allowing them to reproduce more. You get a good source of prebiotics when you eat fruits, vegetables, nuts, and seeds!

If you take antibiotics, they may kill the good and bad bacteria, but they don't kill off yeast. In your colon, you have a balance between yeast and bacteria. Yeast helps break down carbohydrates, and you need that kind of yeast.

But the yeast is always battling with the bacteria. If you start killing off the bacteria, the yeast starts to multiply. And if it keeps multiplying, it will eventually burrow holes in your small intestine and get into your blood system. We call that a "systemic yeast infection." You might have skin rashes or infections, vaginal yeast infections, jock itch, athlete's foot, or thrush in the mouth.

# The Spit Test

Want a simple way to test whether you might have a yeast infection?

Get a glass of clear water (let's hope the water you're drinking is clear; otherwise, we got biggah problems than this, boys!) and put it next to your bed. When you wake up the next morning, get a big mouthful of saliva and spit into the glass. Okay, I know, it's not very glamorous, but hang with me on this.

If your spit produces what I call "streamers" that look like jellyfish hanging down to the bottom of the glass, you might want to investigate further to see if you have a yeast infection. If the spit just floats on the top, chances are you don't have to worry about a yeast infection. (Note: you might have to wait up to an hour for this to occur. If no streamers form, you are OK.)

If you see streamers, you will want to go to your holistic practitioner or medical doctor for some further testing and recommendations for treatment.

Just one of Dr. Joe's little tricks of the trade!

Yeast infections are difficult to get rid of, but you need to do it because if the yeast gets into your body, it can cause all sorts of problems—emotional problems and physical and digestive issues. A yeast infection is something you do not want to ignore.

The stomach is designed to be very acidic. The rest of the body is designed to be generally more alkaline. So you can have too much acid everywhere else and not enough acid in your stomach.

## The Decline of Stomach Acid

As a general rule, stomach acid levels decrease with the increase in age. If you're a 10-year-old kid, we're going to assume that you have 100 percent of your digestive acids. But by the time you're 60, that percentage is going to be down to about 20 percent of what you had when you were a kid. By the time you're 70, it's going to go down to about 10 percent.

And then as you get older, it gets even less and less. This is one of the things that you have to be on guard about, because some people can essentially starve to death, even if they're eating the right food, as they have always done. That's why it's important to eat raw food. Raw food has enzymes in it that aid digestion.

Here's a gross, but interesting fact. If you're ever in a senior citizen home and it smells like urine, that smell is not necessarily what you think it is. Your body uses minerals like calcium and magnesium to neutralize acids. As you get older, you start to deplete your mineral stores through this process, and eventually your body can't neutralize these acids anymore. So the body is trying to keep itself alive. It's in survival mode and starts to produce ammonia to neutralize the acids.

It's not the most efficient method, but it's the only option your body has. That ammonia odor can actually be released through the skin. So what you smell in nursing homes and senior citizen homes is not actually urine, but the scent of the body trying to neutralize acids.

That's why it's so vital for older people—and all of us—to make sure we're eating foods that are mostly raw and alive.

The digestive system is so vital. And you can do so many things to protect and enhance it just by changing your diet!

# Dr. Joe's Extreme Secrets to Weight Loss

**N**o matter where I go—a party, the grocery store, a football game, a business meeting—people always ask me about all aspects of health. And the one subject that *always* comes up is weight loss.

That's not surprising, since 65 percent of all Americans have some sort of interest in weight loss. You see people all the time sucking down diet drinks and following the latest fad diet, but they're always sick, exhausted—and still overweight.

So, why don't these diet plans work?

Because you have to give your body the tools it needs to build a better, healthier you. And I'm telling you: it can't get the right tools from a daily low-carb, diet-drink-laden menu.

So this chapter will address the questions I hear most often from people who want to lose weight.

# Intermittent Fasting

The number one question is always . . . drum roll, please . . .

*What is the easiest way to lose weight?*

And my answer is: the easiest way I have found for myself, my patients, and clients to lose weight is a practice called intermittent fasting.

Simply put, when you eat a meal, it takes about eight hours for your body to utilize the fuel, or the energy, from that meal. After eight hours, your body starts to look elsewhere for fuel, and that's when it starts to burn fat. During the day, we typically eat about every four to six hours, so our body never truly gets into the fat-burning mode.

If you eat dinner at 5 p.m., by about 1 a.m., your body is looking around and going, "Hey, I need some more fuel here. I need something to burn." That's when it will start to burn fat.

If you eat dinner at 5 p.m. and don't eat anything else until the next morning about 10 a.m., now something really cool will start happening. All of those hours past the eight-hour window have been used to burn fat.

Not only is this tactic good for fat burning, but it's also good for stabilizing blood sugar, which means it's great for diabetics.

If you try this, simply pay attention to how you feel. If you start getting light-headed or foggy, you need to eat something. You might not be able to go 10 or 12 hours without food. Then you have to say, "How far can I go?" Try nine hours. Great! That's one hour of fat burning time!

If you can go from five at night until five in the morning without eating, there's four hours when you're going to burn fat and stabilize your blood sugar. This also helps your brain work more efficiently. But you have to find out what timing works best for you.

So, start by going eight hours without eating. See how you feel. Then try nine hours and keep trying to stretch it a little more each time.

If you can do this, you will be amazed at how much more energy you'll have. Studies have also shown that if you work out on an empty stomach, you'll actually have better results. Try it and see if it works for you! Note: If you have diabetes or adrenal gland problems, talk to your doctor before trying this.

# Food Addiction

I frequently have to talk with people about food addiction. So many people ask me about it that I want to explain a little bit about this subject here.

The key to having sustained energy throughout the day is to maintain a steady level of blood sugar. If you eat a simple carbohydrate without a lot of fiber, the simple carbohydrate (also known as a simple sugar) is quickly absorbed into your blood system.

A large level of sugar floating around in your blood causes the body to release insulin. Insulin has several jobs, one of which is to carry the sugar to the cells where the cells use the sugar as fuel. This big influx of fuel for the cells gives you an energy rush. The problem is, once the rush is over, your blood sugar (your fuel supply) drops and the cells, in a sense, run out of fuel. And you feel tired.

## The Sugar Cycle

You now want a quick "pick-me-up," so you reach for more simple sugar to refuel your cells, and the cycle continues. If we go one step further, we see that if we continue to eat simple sugars, the cells will fill up with fuel and cannot accept any more.

This excess sugar cannot remain in the blood because the sugar is an acid. As we've discussed before, too much acid in the blood is very dangerous. The acid can, in very simple terms, eat little holes in the blood vessels. If you start to develop these holes in your blood vessels, the body must fill in these holes before the blood vessel becomes weak and runs the risk of rupturing.

Here's where the problem comes in: The body fills in these holes with cholesterol. The more holes we have in our blood vessels, the more cholesterol is plastered onto the vessels, and the narrower the blood vessels become. Narrow blood vessels prevent normal levels of blood from properly nourishing the body, and a reduced blood supply will cause parts of the body to malfunction.

The body needs to get the excess sugar out of the blood, so if the cells cannot accept the sugar, the body sends the sugar to the liver where it is converted to glycogen. Glycogen is the way the body stores extra sugar to use as fuel when there is no sugar available in the blood. Glycogen is mainly stored in the liver, under blood vessels, and in muscles. Once all the places to store glycogen are filled up, the body converts glycogen into triglycerides, which are then sent into the blood and stored in the cells as fat. This explains why eating a diet high in simple carbohydrates can cause you to gain weight.

In addition, stored fat in fat cells will cause you to produce more estrogen, which is a growth hormone. Growth hormones do exactly what their name says: cause things to grow. Growth hormones are important, but if you have too many of them, they can cause abnormal growth. One form of abnormal growth is obesity. Another form of abnormal growth is cancer. Pay attention. This is important.

In a strange twist, the more estrogen you have, the more likely you are to lay down fat or—in plain English—gain weight. The more fat you have stored, the more estrogen you will produce, and you get stuck in this vicious cycle. Women, on average, have more estrogen then men, which may be why women often have a tougher time losing weight than men do.

The easiest way not to fall into this fat-storing frenzy is to avoid simple carbohydrates. All of those breads, cookies, cakes, doughnuts, and pastas that you love to eat—not to mention plain old sugar—break down into sugar in your body and turn into fat and make your body acidic.

## Too Few Carbs

After learning this information, many people swing to the other extreme—which is also dangerous. They avoid carbohydrates altogether and rely on a diet of only heavy protein foods.

This eating plan is dangerous for other reasons. Too much protein, especially animal protein (meat and dairy), is not a good source of fuel. The brain runs on glucose (a form of sugar), and high-protein diets are very low in glucose. The brain will try to function on a byproduct of protein and fat, but it does not do a good job with those materials. This explains the "brain fog" many people who are on high-protein diets report.

A sustained release of complex carbohydrates will give the body the fuel it needs to function normally. The way to achieve this is by eating whole foods that are high in fiber.

What are "whole foods," you ask? Whole foods are foods that are eaten in their most natural form. For example:

- "Old fashioned" oatmeal will give you a high-fiber meal, releasing sugar slowly. Instant oatmeal, which is processed and chopped up very finely, will not give you as slow of a release of natural sugars. Groats, which are a wholesome version of oats, are an even better choice.

- Brown rice has all its fiber intact and will not give you a quick rush of sugar. White rice, which is brown rice without the high-fiber

outer-covering bran, will break down into sugar very quickly. This
is one reason why you get hungry not long after a dinner that
includes white rice, even though you ate large servings.

### Cravings

Research has shown that people who eat high-fiber whole foods will
snack up to 35 percent less than those who don't eat high-fiber foods.
Certain foods will cut your cravings and keep you from getting hungry
for hours, while other foods will cause cravings and make you feel
hungry shortly after you eat and should be full.

If you are hungry, you are hungry for nutrients. Food is one way to
get nutrients into our body. Quality supplements are another way we
can get nutrients. If we have enough nutrients, we will be less hungry.
I can safely say that the food addicts I have worked with are malnour-
ished. When food addicts get all the nutrients they need, the cravings
will be curbed or will go away entirely.

## Food Addiction Explained

Research has shown that intake of a few common foods need to be
monitored, and in many cases, totally avoided. Dr. Neal Barnard, in
his book *Breaking the Food Seduction*, writes about the four foods that
can cause a chemical reaction in your brain similar to that caused by
heroin, cocaine, and other addicting drugs:

- Chocolate
- Dairy
- Meat
- Simple sugars

You can form a physical addiction for these foods, and you must
address these addictions if you are to overcome them and return to
good health. These addictions can be as serious as any drug addiction.

Food addictions are treated in similar ways to drug addictions.

Many people will say there is no reason to live if they can't have meat, dairy, simple sugars, or chocolate—even after they are taught why these foods are so dangerous. Really? Your entire life revolves around food? Anybody see a problem with this? Does this sound like other addictions you've heard about?

## Blame It on Our Ancestors

These four foods can have a physical effect on your brain because they stimulate the brain's pleasure center. There are several reasons why meat, simple sugars, dairy, and chocolate have this addictive effect. When the human race did not have access to all the foods that most of us have access to today, it was important to eat to sustain life. Eating had to be pleasurable or we as humans would not have bothered since it was so much trouble to hunt, gather, and prepare the food that had the nutrients we needed.

Even today, eating is an expensive habit, not only financially, but also in time and energy. So in the past, foods that provided the densest concentration of nutrients were in demand because they were cheaper in terms of energy expenditure.

Foods with concentrated proteins, fats, and carbohydrates were at the top of this list. Eating these foods would release chemicals in the brain that provided pleasure, prompting early humans to go out and risk life and limb to get more of them. In the process, our body was nourished and we thrived.

Today, we have relatively easy access to food; however, we still seek out foods high in protein, carbohydrates, and fats. But problems arise when these foods are available in such great abundance and—worse yet—in a processed, concentrated form. If normal amounts of these foods give you a little pleasure, the more processed and concentrated versions of these foods provide even more pleasure, and soon you are addicted to that pleasure.

For example, if the sugar in an apple will give you a slow release of energy and a slight release of pleasure chemicals, apple juice that is concentrated and has added sugar and high fructose corn syrup will give you a *rush* of these pleasure chemicals, and you will want more.

High amounts of pleasure chemicals (neurotransmitters) can override logical thought and cause you to do things you know are logically not right, but the desire to "get high" can lead you to do things that are not in your best interest.

You might have experienced this when you were presented with a chocolate brownie with ice cream. You know that if you eat all of it, you will feel sick and/or gain weight, but you do it anyway. When you are done, you feel awful and wonder why you did it. You swear you will never do it again, but the next time you are in a similar situation, you become weak, give in, and do it again.

## Ramping Up the Addictive Qualities

Now imagine what a great high you will get if we concentrate sugar, add it to white flour (which quickly converts into sugar), add a concentrated protein—let's say an egg—and top it off with a concentrated fat, such as butter. Now we have a piece of cake, pie, or bread. If you are prone to food addiction, even the mention of these foods will likely make your mouth water, and you will go out of your way in time, energy, or money to get these items.

You or someone you know most likely has a food addiction and will act around concentrated foods the way a drug addict or alcoholic will act around drugs or alcohol. You may have never considered this effect of food on your body.

According to research by Dr. David Perlmutter, MD, scientists at Connecticut College discovered that Oreos stimulate a rat's brain in a way similar to most drugs. Chemicals in gluten and wheat stimulate the same parts of the brain that are responsive to morphine. Sugar is one of the Seven Deadly Sins that people really struggle with, due to its addictive nature.

How do these foods actually act on your body?

When a food gives you pleasure, a chemical called dopamine is produced and released. Dopamine acts on the part of your brain that stores memories, so a good memory is then associated with this food that created pleasure. Your body then comes to expect pleasure, and you will seek out this food to experience pleasure again.

Certain things we put in our body will stimulate the pleasure centers in the brain beyond the level of even concentrated foods. Drugs such as heroin, cocaine, alcohol, marijuana, and even some prescription drugs can have this pleasurable effect on the brain.

Some people's brains will be more stimulated by a certain food, drug, or experience than others. That's why one person might be susceptible to becoming a food addict, while another person might be susceptible to drugs or alcohol, and another may not have an addiction reaction to any of these. Some people will develop a physical dependency on certain chemicals, which will cause withdrawal symptoms if they do not get a regular "fix" of the chemical.

## Breaking Free

In theory, any food can produce stimulating chemicals. However, it is clear that meat, dairy, concentrated sugar, chocolate, and similar foods are more stimulating than others. Like certain drugs, these foods can put your brain into overload.

The only way to avoid an eating binge is to avoid the foods that cause the chemical reactions in your brain. If you have a sugar addiction, avoid all processed, low-fiber sugars. If it's meat or dairy or chocolate that gives you a problem, you must avoid these types of food.

It will take several days for you to get over the cravings, but if you avoid these foods for several months, you might be able to eat small quantities again without the addiction reaction. That being said, there is no reason for you to ever go back to eating meat, dairy, sugar, or chocolate. All these foods are counterproductive to your goal of good health. There are over 120,000 foods that will take you to your goal of good health, so there is no need to reintroduce bad foods into your diet after you've overcome these difficult habits.

It is easy to see whether a food causes you to have a reaction. If you can eat just a small portion of a specific food and walk away without any cravings, you most likely don't have an addiction. If you can't walk away because you do have cravings, you most likely have an addiction.

Now that you understand *why* you haven't been able to give up certain foods, you can address the issue and deal with it. You can give up the bad foods, replace them with good foods such as fruits, vegetables, raw nuts, and raw seeds, and move quickly toward optimum health.

By not poisoning yourself, eating right, and keeping the nervous system working properly, you really can be one of those amazingly, disgustingly, and extremely healthy people! And slim too!

# Perceiving Stimulation

According to recent research, there seems to be a relationship between the numbers of opiate receptor sites a person has in their brain and how susceptible that person is to becoming an addict. An opiate receptor site is the area in the brain that picks up stimulating chemicals such as dopamine and causes you to feel pleasure.

If a person has fewer opiate receptor sites, they need more stimulation in order to get the same pleasure experience as someone who has more opiate receptor sites. The more stimulants taken in, the more side effects that person is likely to have.

In order for someone who is low in opiate receptor sites to get an "acceptable" amount of pleasure, they need to overload on stimulants—and the effects can be devastating.

# Dr. Joe's Secrets to Extreme Exercise

So why should I exercise? Everybody talks about exercise. It seems like every third commercial on TV is about exercise; one of the three is for prescription drugs, and the other one is for bad food. Of course, you need to take the drugs because you're not exercising and you're not eating right! But that's not what you will be doing when you finish this book, is it?

So, let's talk about exercise. Why should we even do anything? Well, the heart pumps blood to the body, so we have to keep that muscle healthy. How do we do that? Diet and exercise.

In addition to your blood-pumping heart, you have two other circulation paths that move through the body; these are called the lymphatic system. Lymphatics filter out things like germs, bacteria, and pathogens; then they break them down and flush them out of your system. If you've ever had a sore throat and noticed that the glands in your neck are also swollen, you've seen your lymphatic glands at work. Why? You have a big infection, and they are working, filtering out the infection.

The only thing that makes the lymphatic system pump is muscle contraction. You have to keep the muscles contracting to flush out the lymphatic system, so your immune system can fight off the bad guys and keep your body healthy. You've probably never looked at exercise as a way to keep your body healthy! You thought it was just to lose weight or build muscles!

# Feed Your Head

In addition, there is another reason to exercise that almost nobody talks about: exercise stimulates the sacro-occipital pump. *The what?* Your brain and your spinal cord float in a substance called cerebrospinal fluid; this fluid nourishes the brain and spinal cord and also acts as a cushion for both. And this fluid relies on the sacro-occipital pump to get it where it needs to go.

It's a mechanical pump system comprised of your sacrum, which is your tailbone—a triangular-shaped bone in the middle of your spine right below your belt-line (the low end of the pump)—and your occiput—the back part of your skull (which serves as the top end of the pump). Every time you inhale, the sacrum and the occiput drop down, and every time you exhale, the sacrum and occiput rise, and this action pumps cerebrospinal fluid mechanically through your spine and your brain. Think of the sacrum and occiput working together to pump the fluid through your spine and brain.

When you're walking and breathing, you're pumping the cerebrospinal fluid. So, if you are exercising, you're probably moving more and breathing more, which means you're pumping more cerebrospinal fluid. If you're sitting down all day in your job, or if you drive a lot, you're not moving the sacro-occipital pump, and you're depriving your brain and spinal cord of fresh infusions of the proper amount of cerebrospinal fluid. Exercise makes this pump work.

If the bones in your lower back or pelvis move out of place, and if you have back, hip, sciatic, or sacroiliac pain, it could be a sign that your sacrum is out of place and not pumping properly. If you have headaches, especially at the base of your skull, it could be a sign that the oxygen is not pumping properly to the brain. The sacro-occipital pump is extremely important to make sure that your brain is getting enough oxygen.

Through chiropractic adjustments, most times, we can actually put the bones back in place to get the sacro-occipital pump working again. In my office, we have special tables to help pump the cerebrospinal fluid. So, even if you use a wheelchair most of the time, there are still therapies that can help you move this fluid.

# Rocking Horse Therapy

There's a thing called equestrian therapy, which is often very effective for children who have certain learning and physical disabilities. The children are put on a horse, and the horse is led around with the child in the saddle, and as the children are riding, they are rocking back and forth.

Some research shows equestrian therapy is actually helping the children's brains function more efficiently. One reason is because the rocking motion is mechanically manipulating the sacro-occipital pump so that more cerebrospinal fluid is moving through their spine and brain.

If your sacrum is out of place, it may not be pumping the cerebrospinal fluid properly—another reason to get your spine checked on a regular basis by your highly qualified, friendly neighborhood chiro-practor! Few medical orthopedists perform these types of checks.

# High Intensity Interval Training

Regular weight-bearing exercise and flexibility training are vital to improving health and preventing disease. You don't have to look like Arnold Schwarzenegger in his prime, but maintaining good muscle tone and flexibility helps enhance your body's well-being and prevents arthritis, osteoporosis, and a host of other ailments.

To get into an exercise habit, you need to find something you enjoy. Personally, I'm an outdoors guy. I like to hike, climb, rollerblade, partic-ipate in water sports—but that's me. You've got to find what works for you. There are plenty of books, gyms, personal trainers, and DVD series out there to help you, but I'd like to make a few of my own recommendations.

The first is something called high intensity interval training (HIIT). Bodybuilders used this technique years ago, and it is now being brought back into the light of day by, of all people, research scientists, not the exercise industry. This training puts a lot of stress on your body for a very short period of time, which is followed by an interval of rest.

Here's an example of a HIIT workout:

- Warm up for two to three minutes.
- Run, bike, row—or perform any other aerobic activity—as hard as you can for about 20 to 30 seconds.
- Slow your pace but don't stop for 90 seconds.
- Repeat this "fast–slow" cycle eight times.

It's easy to perform this kind of cycle on an elliptical machine, but I wouldn't recommend trying it on a treadmill because you might not be able to change speeds quickly enough. Also, if you are short on workout time, you can cut the rest time to 10 seconds and have your eight sets done in four or five minutes.

In my opinion, the best thing about HIIT is that you are completely done in about 20 minutes, and you only have to do this twice a week. Any more often could be too much stress on your body.

I have shared this technique with many of my friends, from "weekend warriors" to professional athletes, and all who have tried it have been amazed at their results. Some of these people are "professional exercisers," for lack of a better term, and they say they are losing weight and feeling better using this type of workout. It has even worked better for some of them than long-distance running, which has actually been proven to be very stressful on the body in a negative way—speeding up the aging process and increasing risk for certain health problems.

## HGH Booster

HIIT also boosts the level of human growth hormone (HGH) in the body. HGH is produced by the pituitary gland and is a naturally occurring substance in your body.

Whenever you put something synthetic in the body, it's not going to be as good as the stuff you make yourself. And in fact, everybody produces their own special formula of hormones, so my hormones are slightly different than the hormones of the guy next to me. If you're trying to boost hormones, you want the best hormones you can get—the stuff you produce yourself. HIIT training is one of the few workouts that actually increases HGH levels.

You want to get the HGH level up and let your body maintain it for a few hours, but if you eat sugar after a workout like HIIT, you're going to slow down your production of HGH. So, no sugar for at least two or three hours after this type of workout, although proteins or fats are fine. A salad with raw organic apple cider vinegar dressing will help keep your energy level up and your body alkaline, which is important because exercise creates a lot of acid waste in the body. Also good are peas, nuts, or seeds. But NO sugar of any kind—not even sports drinks or fruit for at least two to three hours.

Have a salad after your workout; include some nutritional yeast, hemp, or chia seeds (both high in omega-3 fatty acids and protein) and use your raw organic apple cider vinegar as a dressing. That will give you an amazing source of energy for your body that's easily digestible and includes tons of nutrients, and you'll feel great! (Nutritional yeast is yellow and looks like mashed potatoes. It is loaded with B vitamins, proteins, and good fats—and it tastes great.)

# An Instant Energy Boost

Most people would like more energy, right? I'm going to tell you about an exercise that can instantly give you more energy. After I've described it, take a little a break from reading—especially if you've been sitting for a while and are feeling a little overwhelmed by all of the information I've shared—and try out this technique.

But first, I need to teach you a little bit of advanced neurology. This is neat stuff. It's how the brain works. Now I think we all know that the right side of the brain controls the left side of your body and the left side of the brain controls the right side of your body.

Most of us, all day, every day, use one side of our body more than we use the other. We favor that side of our body when we work our mouse, brush our teeth, zip our fly, drive our car, and operate a spoon. Which means we're using one side of our brain more than the other—all day, every day.

Your brain is designed to be integrated, not segregated. But when we spend all day, every day using one side, we are forcing our brain to be segregated. And so by the end of the day, our brain short-circuits.

So I'm going to teach you a quick little exercise that can actually improve your cognitive function, your memory, your energy level, and your coordination. It only takes 30 seconds, and you can do it anywhere. Ready to learn it?

It's called a cross crawl, and it forces us to use both sides of our brain at the same time.

## Wake Up Your Nervous System

A cross crawl is such a powerful exercise because it actually "recalibrates" your neurology. You can do cross crawls at any time, but you should especially try them first thing in the morning, because they stimulate the sympathetic nervous system.

There are two types of nerves in the body, a system that speeds you up and another that slows you down. The "speed-up" system is called sympathetic; the parasympathetic system slows you down. When you get out of bed in the morning, you are in a parasympathetic mode, that "slow down," groggy place. But you can actually kick-start your sympathetic nervous system by doing something like a cross crawl.

Getting your sympathetic nervous system going will give you energy, brain clarity, and more importantly, speed up your metabolism. That's why working out is important, but working out in the morning is even better. If you work out in the morning, you become a fat-burning machine.

Stand up straight, then lift your left leg and raise your right arm. Now put them down and lift your left arm and your right leg, and then put them down. It's like marching in place!

When you first starting doing cross crawls, it will feel weird, but it should feel completely natural very quickly—probably in under a minute. You should do this exercise at a comfortable pace for 30 seconds three times a day. Easy cheesy. Vegan cheesy, of course!

## If Your Brain Is Switched

Now some people can't do the cross crawl. If they can't, I consider the possibility that their "brain is switched." If you can't do this or if this doesn't come naturally to you, focus on touching your left knee to your right elbow, and touch your left elbow to your right knee.

Even this might be challenging for some people, but it's important for you to work on it. Focus on getting your left elbow to your right knee and your right elbow to your left knee. By doing this, you're going to be able to reboot your brain, although it will take some some time and will feel awkward at first.

Why do people lose this ability? What happens? Certain events, habits, or accidents can short-circuit the brain. It could be a chemical reaction; it could be a physical condition; or it could be from head trauma. But we want to try to get the brain rewired.

Years ago they told us once a brain cell is dead, it's dead forever. Well, it turns out, that's actually wrong. We've learned that some brain cells can regenerate themselves at an amazing rate. And sometimes when the brain can't regenerate itself, it can rewire itself around the damaged area. This is referred to as neuroplasticity.

So the body can actually heal the brain, which is why people who have strokes can recover some or all of their functions. Rehabilitation can help the brain heal or rewire itself, and when you do these exercises, you are rebooting your brain.

Sometimes your computer just doesn't work, and what will be the first thing your IT person will tell you to do? Just reboot it. I don't know why rebooting works for my computer. I just know that it usually does.

So, that's what we'll do for your brain. Just reboot it. Then it works better.

OK, so now I want you to put the book down, get up, and do the cross crawl for 30 seconds. We're going to march right arm, left leg, left arm, right leg. Or do the alternative exercise: right elbow to left knee; left elbow to right knee. Don't forget to come back when you're done!

## It's Better to Crawl Before You Walk

As an infant, it's a natural thing to allow a baby to crawl. If you put a baby down and they can't crawl, right arm, left leg, left arm, right leg and they start crawling unilaterally, right arm, right leg, left arm, left leg, that could be a sign that the brain is not functioning as well as it should.

So, a little trick you can do if you have a child that can't do that, or if you have an older person that can't do it: Lay them on their back and have somebody grab the right arm and left leg and another person reach over from the other side, grab their right arm and left leg, and you mimic that cross crawling motion for them laying on their back. And that too can help reboot or rewire the brain. It's important that a child does crawl. Some people say, "Well, my child went from lying in a crib directly to walking." That's not really something to brag about. It may not be the best for the child never to have crawled. You want the child to crawl around because it helps build up the nervous system. The second thing crawling does for a child is that as the child is lying on their belly they lift their head up, and as they lift their head up they start to form what's called the "cervical curve," which is the curve in the neck.

You should have about a 60-degree curve in your neck. A 60 curve allows for the strongest neck you can possibly have with the maximum amount of flexibility.

Most people, at some time in their lives, lose the curvature in their neck, or the curve never formed at all (remember the baby NOT crawling?) If you don't have the curve in your neck, the spine will wear out and that leads to osteoarthritis. So, a neck with the curve most likely won't get arthritis, and a neck without a curve will. So it's vital that the baby be allowed to lie on their belly and lift their head up so that they can form that natural, cervical curve so that they have a normal, healthy neck as they get older.

# Other Exercise Tools

I'd like to talk about the use of a piece of fitness equipment I call a rebounder, which can add to your overall health and feeling of wellness. No, a rebounder is not someone you date after a crushing breakup. A rebounder is a mini-trampoline that you can keep in your home. Using one can help stimulate your lymph nodes. It's very simple—you jump on the rebounder; it stimulates your sympathetic nervous system.

If you don't have time for a full workout in the morning, you can do cross crawls on the rebounder. Thirty seconds of that will start stimulating your sympathetic nerves, which will increase your metabolism rate and create energy to get your brain working clearer. A rebounder can also help your digestion because jumping up and down is going to help stimulate your bowels, which can help you get rid of a lot of toxins and poisons first thing in the morning.

And working out on rebounders can stimulate your lymphatic system. Bouncing up and down on the rebounder will stimulate the lymphatics to flush themselves out because you're contracting your muscles. You're getting a double whammy doing the cross crawl on a mini-trampoline.

### Stepping Out

There's also a good method for getting exercise by measuring your daily steps. Buy yourself a pedometer and record how many steps you take in a day. Your goal should be to take 10,000 steps a day. Ten thousand steps a day is equivalent to a 20-minute aerobic workout.

So get your pedometer, wear it for five days, and figure out how many steps you typically take a day. The average person takes about 5,000 to 6,000 steps a day. When you start trying to get to 10,000 steps per day, you will find yourself looking for ways to increase the number of steps you take. You can do this by parking farther away from store entrances and taking the stairs instead of elevators.

At the end of the day, if you notice that you haven't gotten in your steps, you'll be motivated to keep walking. It really is the easiest, quickest way to have a low-stress workout.

# Easing the Pain

You might be avoiding working out because you always get hurt when you start a new exercise plan. But did you know that what you eat can determine how much pain you feel when the body is injured? Certain foods will facilitate the healing process, while others can actually exacerbate a painful condition.

Omega-6 fatty acids are necessary for normal hormone production and proper cellular function. Another essential fatty acid is known as omega-3. The average American takes in much more omega-6 than omega-3 fatty acids. When the body has an excess amount of omega-6 fatty acids, it will convert those excess acids into prostaglandin E2, which causes inflammation that can irritate nerves and increase pain. Prostaglandin E2 is the biological equivalent of putting gasoline on a fire. Ouch. But as you increase your intake of omega-3 fatty acids, they will block the chain of events that cause inflammation and thus cause a decrease in pain.

*"So, Dr. Joe, you are telling me that I can actually reduce pain levels by changing the way I eat?"*

That would be an emphatic *"Yes, sir!"*

The problem in the standard American diet is that we eat way too much of the bad fats and not nearly enough of the good fats. By decreasing the amounts of omega-6 fatty acids you consume and increasing the amount of omega-3 fatty acids you take in, you can in fact reduce pain levels in your body. There are enzymes in the body called cox enzymes that facilitate inflammation. Some inflammation is a good thing. If you sprain your ankle, you need inflammation to protect your joints; if a bee stings you, the inflammation helps to contain the poison from the sting. However, too much inflammation causes pain and is one of the contributing components to conditions such as fibromyalgia.

Omega-3 fatty acids block the cox enzymes in a way very much like many pain-killing medications do. Once the cox enzymes are blocked, inflammation is greatly limited, and thus the pain is extremely reduced or eliminated.

The sources of omega-6 fatty acids may be surprising. Corn oil, sunflower oil, safflower oil, cottonseed oil, and even soybean oil have a very high omega-6 fatty acid content relative to their omega-3 fatty acid levels. Other sources of omega-6 fatty acids are meat and dairy products.

Good sources of omega-3 fatty acids are flaxseed oil, walnut oil, and evening primrose oil. Another very good source of omega-3 fatty acids is fish oil. However, there is a major downside to consuming fish oil because many of them contain mercury, a highly toxic metal. Mercury waste by-products produced by man are often dumped into the waters. Bacteria consume these waste products, and then small fish consume the bacteria. Larger fish will in turn eat the smaller fish. This is how mercury gets up the food chain into fish oil.

Another possible downside is that not all fish oil contains high levels of omega-3 fatty acids. Omega-3 fatty acids come from algae. Small fish eat the algae, which contain the omega-3 fatty acids; bigger fish eat the small fish, and still bigger fish eat them. Farm-raised fish do not consume algae by eating smaller algae-eating fish, so they do not contain significant levels of omega-3 fatty acids.

Plant sources of omega-3s come in a form called ALA, which has to be converted into DHA and EPA form. A healthy body should be able to do this. However, most people aren't healthy enough to provide that conversion, so if you want a good source of DHA and EPA, eat what the fish eat! Take omega-3 supplements made from algae. This form of omega-3s is more expensive, but it's worth it!

# Final Exercise Secrets

Exercise is a very good way to enhance the immune system; however, recent studies have shown that too much exercise can have a reverse effect on the immune system's ability to help keep us disease-free. Low to moderate exercise will help build and maintain the immune system.

Walking is one of the best forms of exercise. It is low impact on the joints, can be done just about anywhere by just about anyone, and not only helps the body but also creates endorphins in the brain, which are chemicals that make you feel good.

Too much exertion actually lowers the ability of the body to fight disease and leaves us susceptible to attack from bacteria and other microorganisms. Too much exercise will also create free radicals, which are molecules that attack the cells in the body and can cause the cells to weaken or even die. If free radicals attack the DNA of cells, it can cause them to mutate and can lead to cancer.

Exercising three times a week for 20 minutes a day will do the body good. It is also better to exercise regularly, even if only for a short period of time, than it is to work out very hard, but only once in a while. A few minutes a day or every other day is better than one hour once a week.

Remember, there are three things that nerves need: oxygen, stimulation, and nutrition. So if a nerve is being pinched, it's not getting the proper stimulation, and exercise can sometimes help alleviate this problem. Oxygen is obviously brought into the body through breathing, and when you exercise, you breathe more.

When it comes to exercise, the secret is doing something that you like. I can sit here and tell you that you need to do this four-minute exercise or eight minutes of that exercise, or that you need to do aerobics, or you need to do weight training, or take 10,000 steps a day. But you're not going to do it if you don't like it.

You've got to find out what works for you.

There are certain exercises I don't like. If I jump rope, it gives me a headache. I won't jump rope, but that doesn't mean *you* shouldn't jump rope. Try different things and find out what works for you.

And remember this good rule about exercise: if it hurts, stop now. Let me clarify what I mean by that.

If you're working out, your muscles are going to be sore from time to time. But if you're working out and you feel like your shoulder is going to come out of the socket, or you're getting a blazing headache, or numbness is tingling down your leg, that's not right. You could be causing more neurological damage if you're exercising in the wrong way. So, if it hurts, you should stop.

I want you to build strong muscles around straight bones. I don't want you building strong muscles around crooked bones. So if you're having joint pains—numbness and tingling—get the joints checked to make sure they're not out of alignment. If they are, put the bones back in place and unpinch the nerves.

The more you exercise, the better you will get at it. It's just the nature of the beast. So if you like walking three minutes a day, then swing your arms left and right as you walk. Do the cross crawl and walk three minutes a day and then you're going to find the extra three minutes to exercise. You start to feel good. It's the reward you get for taking the time to exercise.

Walking is usually going to be your best friend. But if you don't want to walk, I recommend that you start with a yoga class. A beginner yoga class is great. It increases circulation and helps flexibility. You can build up from there.

If you like swimming, just make sure you shower with a natural nontoxic soap such as castile soap as soon as you get out of a chlorine pool. Chlorine is a highly toxic gas; we used it to kill our enemies in the Vietnam War, and now we put it in swimming pools. Go figure.

CHAPTER 9

# Now What?

After learning most of the information that I have shared with you in this book, many people look at me and say two words: Now what?

This chapter will help you move from sitting and reading into action mode. I'm giving you some strategies you can use on a daily basis to start down the secret path to extreme health.

Here are a few simple tips for you to digest (no pun intended) and to get you moving (again, no pun intended).

## Water

Yes, I know. You've heard it until you're sick of it. But it is true. Water truly is the elixir of life. The trick is to drink plenty of pure water.

When I get tired of the same old, same old, one of my favorite tricks is to add a little bit of cinnamon to my water. It provides a little variety to the routine. Cinnamon also helps stabilize your blood sugar and stabilize your energy levels throughout the day.

I recommend that you always use organic herbs or spices. Nonorganic spices can be irradiated, which means that they are zapped with radiation to help kill off viruses, germs, bacteria, and other creepy crawlies. Most people generally don't want to "belly up to the bar" and order a cup of radiation. Plus, some research shows that radiation alters the quality of the spices.

When it comes to water, the most practical type of water you can drink would be reverse osmosis water. We talked about this in chapter 2, so you can turn back there for more details. I think reverse osmosis is probably the user-friendliest "good water" you can drink. I personally drink reverse osmosis water.

Glass containers are the best way to store and transport your water. The good news is that a lot of manufacturers have caught on to this secret and are making glass containers with plastic housings to protect the glass. Your next-best choice would be stainless steel.

If you have to use plastic, harder plastic is better than the softer plastic. However, both hard and soft plastics begin to break down when they get hot, and they leach chemicals into the water, such as xenoestrogens (*xeno* means foreign). These foreign estrogens can be hundreds of times stronger than human estrogen. Estrogen is a growth hormone. Most of us are done with our "growing up." So, if we're not growing up, we're growing out. Estrogen causes you to lay down fat.

If you have water in plastic bottles, whatever you do, don't let it sit in your car on a hot day. If you take a drink of water out of a plastic bottle and it tastes funky, throw it away immediately.

Your best bet is to invest in a whole-house water filter so that even your toilet water is clean. Why is that important? If your water has chlorine, and it sits in your toilet bowl, the chlorine gas evaporates and gets into the air that you're breathing.

Your body is 70 to 80 percent water. It's vital to have pure water in order to obtain and maintain extreme health.

# Fresh Fruit

As I discussed earlier in the book, you should limit your fruit consumption to two or three pieces a day. Don't juice your fruit, unless you're using just a small amount as a flavoring for green veggies. Look back to chapter 6 for my guidelines on juicing.

Make sure that any fruit juice or dried fruit you are eating is not laden with sugar coating or added sugar. And WHATEVER you do, don't consume grocery store fruit juices, fruit boxes, or anything that isn't fresh squeezed!

## Watermelon Love

Fun fact: watermelon contains something called citrolene. Citrolene helps the body produce nitric oxide, which is a vasodilator. A vasodilator helps open up your blood vessels to increase circulation to all parts of your body, including your brain and, yes, even your "love muscles."

Here are some basic guidelines for avoiding pesticides when you're purchasing and consuming fruit, as outlined by the Environmental Working Group. They've rated the dirtiest and cleanest fruits and veggies you can purchase, labeling them the "Dirty Dozen" and the "Clean 15."

The "Dirty Dozen" includes:

1. Strawberries
2. Apples
3. Nectarines
4. Peaches
5. Celery
6. Grapes
7. Cherries
8. Spinach
9. Tomatoes
10. Sweet bell peppers
11. Cherry tomatoes
12. Cucumbers

Now for the "Clean 15":

1. Avocados
2. Sweet corn (but you have to be careful of corn since 94 percent is genetically modified!)
3. Pineapples
4. Cabbage
5. Sweet peas (frozen)
6. Onions
7. Asparagus
8. Mangos
9. Papayas
10. Kiwi
11. Eggplant
12. Honeydew melon
13. Grapefruit
14. Cantaloupe
15. Cauliflower

## Avoiding Pesticides

If you're going to eat the skin of a particular kind of fruit, it's GOT to be organic. Let's use apples as an example. A commercial apple is often sprayed with pesticides, then dipped in wax to give it that really shiny coat. The wax will seal in the pesticides. So washing it will have very little effect on reducing the pesticides on the apple. If you have to eat a nonorganic fruit, make sure you peel it first.

You can buy fruit and vegetable washers, but remember that bottle of raw organic apple cider in your pantry? Add half a cup of that to a gallon of water to wash your fruits and veggies. It's a heck of a lot cheaper than the products they sell in the stores. Submerge your fruits and veggies in the cider water, swish them around, and let them soak for about five minutes. Then lift them out of the water and put them in a strainer or colander and rinse them. When you are washing your fruits and veggies, the dirt and junk settles to the bottom of the water. If you dump the water back over the fruits and veggies, you dump the junk back on it.

# Fresh Vegetables

One piece of advice that I tell all my clients and patients: eat vegetables as often as you can, in as many ways as you can. Put them in salads or sandwiches. Use sprouts and sea vegetables. Buy a steamer, which will save you time and effort in cooking veggies! (One of my patients, who HATES to cook, says that her vegetable steamer is the best investment she's ever made 'cause she can't burn or overcook anything in a steamer!)

Buy organic vegetables as often as possible. Remember—Poison was a 1980s rock band, not what you want to put into your body!

# Nuts and Seeds

Make like a squirrel and store up a stash of nuts and seeds to nibble on. These are a lifesaver when you're traveling and need a quick snack or if you like to have something at your desk to nibble on. Store them in glass jars to keep them fresh.

Consider stocking your pantry with these goodies:

- Raw sunflower seeds (baseball players have known this trick for years!)
- Flaxseeds
- Pumpkin seeds
- Natural nut butters made from almonds, cashews, or other nuts
- Coconut milk and almond milk (some research shows that kids actually prefer almond milk over cow's milk on cereal!)

# Peanuts—the Non-Nut

Nuts are great—almonds, pistachios, filberts, Brazil nuts; the list goes on and on. But did you know that peanuts are not nuts? Peanuts are legumes. Most peanuts, with the exception of Valencia peanuts, contain mycotoxins (which we covered in chapter 5 in the section on coffee). Mycotoxins are harmful chemicals produced by a certain species of fungi. These mycotoxins can cause major allergic reactions and damage the immune system in many people. This is one reason you want to avoid peanut butter.

Another reason to avoid peanut butter is that lot of them have added hydrogenated oil and sugar. Hydrogenated oil is linked to heart disease and can cause inflammation. Peanuts are high in omega-6 fatty acids, which can increase inflammation, which can increase pain.

Peanuts are also high in an amino acid called arginine, which can be good because it helps the body to produce nitric oxide, the vasodilator mentioned above. However, if you have the herpes virus in your body, and a majority of Americans do, it can stimulate the virus to cause outbreaks.

During baseball season, patients will come in and say, "Every time I go to an Atlanta Braves game, I get a herpes outbreak." Well, going to the baseball game didn't cause the outbreak; more than likely, peanuts did. People like to eat peanuts at baseball games, even if they might not normally consume them at other times or other events.

# Supplements

Several years ago, someone came up to me after a lecture and asked, "Dr. Joe, what do you think would be the ultimate supplement in the world to put into your body?" I thought for a second and then answered, "If someone could take raw fruits and vegetables and put them into a pill, that would be the ultimate supplement for everyone to take because that is the ultimate and essential source of nutrition—fruits, vegetables, nuts and seeds."

Later I wondered, "Could *I* really put that type of supplement into a pill?" I began to research the subject and discovered that putting those ingredients into a pill form would be too limiting. But if we created a powder of raw fruits and vegetables, then we could have the world's ultimate supplement.

So I began work to create Dr. Joe's Essential Source for my patients who wanted the "ultimate supplement."

We take raw fruits and vegetables and juice them. Then we take the water out of the juice at a very low temperature, leaving a powder. Then we add prebiotics (defined as a nondigestible food ingredient that promotes the growth of beneficial microorganisms in the intestines), probiotics (a dietary supplement containing live bacteria or yeast that supplements normal gastrointestinal flora, given especially after depletion of flora caused by infection or ingestion of an antibiotic), and a complete multivitamin. There you have the ingredients of Dr. Joe's Essential Source.

The name Essential Source refers to the raw fruits and vegetables that are the basis for the product. Raw fruits and vegetables ARE the "essential source" that all humans need to have a healthy body. This is where you should get your nutrients—from the essential sources of raw fruits and vegetables.

Dr. Joe's Essential Source is a convenient, energizing, all-natural vegetarian formula that is suitable for the whole family. The formula contains a complete multivitamin complex, a rich sea vegetable complex, and several fruit and vegetable extracts. This formulation delivers a full spectrum of antioxidants, enzymes, and probiotics. It provides digestive and immune support, fiber, and acts as an appetite suppressant while keeping blood sugar balanced.

Essential Source is safe for diabetics and contains no gluten, sugars, artificial sweeteners, colors, flavors, corn, wheat, yeast, eggs, or preservatives.

## Super Greens

After I developed Essential Source, I remained troubled by the fact that so many people were still eating bad diets. One of the biggest side effects of a bad diet is that your body becomes acidic. You need alkaline products to offset the acids, although you must keep the correct balance.

So I started thinking, "What are some of the most alkalizing, most nutritious foods in the world?" And the answer was things like wheat grass, barley grass, and alfalfa grass. So I created a new supplement with these grasses at the base. We use the same process as with Essential Source—we juice the grasses and take the water out at a very low temperature to make a powder. Then we add omega-3 fatty acids in the form of chlorella and spirulina—two types of algae, which you will remember from the previous chapter are a great source of omega-3.

We then add the algae powder to the wheat, barley, and alfalfa grasses. And then we add dulse—a seaweed—to give you an extra source of iodine, which helps your thyroid and just about every other cell in your body work more efficiently. Most people don't get enough iodine in their diet, and most people don't know that the best iodine comes from sea vegetables.

Mix all those ingredients together, and you get Dr. Joe's Super Greens.

Juicing the vegetables breaks down their cell walls, which we discussed in chapter 6. Then the water is removed at approximately 78 degrees to ensure the product does not lose any nutrients. This leaves a powder, which is very easy for my patients to use.

I recommend mixing one scoop of Essential Source with water or your favorite nondairy milk, such as coconut or raw almond, until completely dissolved, and drink one to three servings per day. For the Super Greens, I recommend two scoops per day mixed with water or a nondairy milk.

Many of my patients mix the Essential Source and the Super Greens together and knock back their morning energy cocktail for the day! It's easy and convenient and gives you a great whole food supplement from the richest whole food sources on the planet.

## Drink Up!

You should drink your glass of Essential Source or Super Greens as soon as possible after you mix it. If you let it stand too long, the nutrients in the formulas will oxidize and break down. It's still great, but not as great as if you drink it right away.

Your supplements should come from whole food ingredients, not synthetic ones, which can cause damage to the body. Essential Source and Super Greens provide that for you in a simple and easy-to-use powder form.

Supplements can be a great way to ensure that your body is getting all the nutrients it needs. In today's busy lifestyles, supplements can be an "easy fix" for correcting some of your less-than-stellar food choices.

# Dr. Joe's Nutrition Kitchen Essentials—What to Keep and What to Toss from Your Pantry!

Keep a variety of these items in your pantry, refrigerator, and freezer so you will always have ingredients on hand to prepare healthy, tasty meals that also fulfill your nutritional needs. I've broken these down first by categories.

### Grains

Keep different types of rice such as brown, basmati, and long grain. Avoid white rice; it's processed and devoid of many natural nutrients. Sorghum, quinoa, millet, corn grits, and wild rice are good staples once you get a little adventurous. I also recommend that you try buckwheat, teff, and nut flours. Keep the grains in a well-sealed glass container, and add a bay leaf to jars in the pantry to help keep the bugs away.

If your pantry is hot, keep your grains in the refrigerator. Label all containers so that you won't forget what you have stored. When you're learning a bunch of new foods, the last thing you need is to have to figure out whether that's the quinoa or the millet in that jar. In addition to labeling the grains, take a minute and write out basic directions for their preparation and tape them to the side of the container or on the inside of the lid. When brown rice takes 50 minutes to prepare and couscous takes five, it's a good idea not to get the two confused. Grains break down to sugar, so if you use them at all, use them sparingly.

## Beans and Legumes

Chickpeas, pinto beans, Great Northern beans, cannellini beans, green and yellow split peas, red and brown lentils, and black beans are all excellent choices to add to your diet, providing high levels of protein and fiber, and giving you the "full" feeling you were accustomed to when you were a meat eater. Place beans and legumes in sealed containers, preferably glass, label them, and store in a cool dry place.

## Pasta

Keep on hand rice pasta and quinoa pasta, all of which come in a variety of shapes and colors and have wonderfully interesting textures and flavors. Processed white flours, which are used to make most conventional stiff, plastic-wrapped pastas, are not digested well and can cause a runny nose, mucus in the body, gas, and fatigue—while draining your body of vital nutrients. Even if you do not have an adverse reaction to wheat, these other pastas are tastier and much more fun. Store pasta in a cool dry place in well-sealed containers. Pastas break down into sugars, so if you use them at all, use them sparingly.

## Sea Veggies

Dulse and nori—yes, they're seaweed—are great seasonings for salad, soups, and dressings, as well as popcorn, potatoes, stir-fries, and beans. Not used to eating seaweed? Think again. Within kelp—the "monster" seaweed that blankets large sections of the ocean floor—is a sticky gum-like substance called algin that ends up in hundreds of foods as a thickener, along with many other products. Algin keeps ice cream creamy and improves the smoothness and texture of cake frosting. Thanks to algin in salad dressing, the oil and vinegar stay together a lot longer. Algin puts the "glaze" in glazed doughnuts, makes milkshakes velvety, whipped cream silky, and pancake syrup thick. Slow-moving ketchup? Blame it on the algin! Of course, you won't be eating many of those foods anymore, will you?

If you swim in the ocean and eat animals from the ocean, what's the big deal about seaweed? These sea vegetables are slightly salty in flavor and are loaded with nutrients, including vitamin B12. These seasonings may not be part of your menu now, but once you try them, you will most likely make them part of your usual flavor enhancers.

## Nuts and Seeds

Almonds, cashews, pecans, filberts, walnuts, pine nuts, peanuts, sunflower seeds, sesame seeds, and pumpkin seeds are just some of the nutritious selections you have to choose from. Be sure to choose nuts that are raw, since they lose some or all valuable nutrients when they're roasted. Nuts and seeds, once shelled, will last about four to six months if refrigerated, up to one year if frozen.

## Nut and Seed Butters

Almonds, cashews, and sesame (also called tahini) and sunflower seeds make excellent butters. These can be bought commercially or made at home in your blender or food processor. Nut and seed butters require refrigeration after opening and will last up to four months. Make sure they don't contain added sugars.

## Dried Fruits

Raisins, figs, apples, mangos, papayas, dates, bananas, prunes, apricots, pears, peaches, persimmons, pineapples, coconuts, and tomatoes are all great to eat when dried. But avoid those containing sulfites or added sugar. Store dried fruits in airtight glass containers, in a cool, dry place, and they'll keep up to six months. If you prefer, soak fruits in distilled warm water for an hour before eating. This is a nice alternative but certainly isn't necessary. If you want to get real ambitious and have a lot of fun in the process, you can pick up a food dehydrator. Make your own dried fruit, using organic fruit, and then you'll know what you're eating.

## Dried Spices and Herbs

You can avail yourself of basil, bay leaves, red pepper, black pepper, cayenne pepper, poultry seasoning, cilantro, garlic, ginger, oregano, turmeric, rosemary, sage, tarragon, thyme, dill weed, chili powder, chives, cinnamon, nutmeg, paprika, and more to spice up your dishes (no pun intended). Store in a cool, dry, convenient place, in sealed glass containers. Try to use organic spices. Non-organic spices can be irradiated.

## Fats and Oils

Poor fat. What a bad rap it's gotten in the last few years. Sure, on average we Americans consume too much of it, but when we get so obsessed with a low fat or no fat diet, things can get out of hand, and some people have reduced their fat intake to unhealthy levels. Bottom line, we need fats in our diets. There have been many fat-free diets and products made available to the public, and most are, at best, not very healthy, and at worst, downright dangerous.

And by the way, fat-free doesn't mean calorie-free. I have to chuckle—sadly—when I hear stories about people who just plow through a whole box of fat-free cookies in one sitting and excuse themselves by saying, "But they're fat-free!" You've never done that, have you? I don't want to know.

We need fat to produce the walls around our cells, give us energy stores, help insulate the body, make hormones, and perform a host of other functions. There are good fats and bad fats. The bad fats are saturated or hydrogenated fats. If a product says "hydrogenated" or "partially hydrogenated oil," avoid it. These dangerous fats will not only cause hardening of the arteries, but they'll hijack the good fats in your body and use them to transport and metabolize themselves. This could lead to not having enough good fats.

Use organic, unrefined oils purchased in small amounts to avoid spoilage. Keep in a dark place as sunlight can destroy many nutrients in oils. You can keep oil in the refrigerator; although it may become thick and cloudy, the appearance won't affect its quality. The best oils for salads are olive, coconut, and flax. The best oil for very light sautéing, sauces, and salads is coconut oil. When you get brave, try other oils such as sesame, avocado, almond, grape-seed, or sunflower.

## Beverages

Drink naturally caffeine-free herbal teas, coconut milk, rice milk, almond milk, seltzer (not to be confused with club soda, which has quite a bit of unhealthy salt in it), and good old distilled or filtered water. Store teas in a cool, dry place. Once milks are opened, they generally only last a week or two. Remember, if a drink or food smells or tastes bad to you, throw it away immediately.

Prepackaged rice, almond, and coconut milks will last longer in the refrigerator than cow's milk will. And you can store them in your pantry, unrefrigerated, until you open them, which is great if you find a killer deal and want to buy a whole case of the stuff. You'll get used to the new types of milk, and the old cow's milk will not even taste good before long. Try different types of milks to find the ones you like best.

## Salty Seasonings

Himalayan or air-dried sea salt, chickpea miso, coconut aminos, olives. Of these, the chickpea miso needs to be refrigerated, while others can be kept at room temperature.

## *Other Seasonings and Such*

Raw organic apple cider vinegar, salsa, ketchup made without sugar, capers, hot sauce, mustard, lemon juice, lime juice, and vanilla. Store vinegar at room temperature; the others require refrigeration.

## *Must-Haves*

**Assortment of fresh fruits and vegetables.** Think outside the box and add some new ones to your diet. Kale, butternut squash, beets, and sweet potatoes can add a lot of extra flavor and nutrients to your diet.

**Variety of "good" oils.** Good ones to have on hand are olive oil, coconut oil, grape-seed oil, avocado oil, and sesame oil. These are great items to use for salad dressings, baking, and sautéing.

**Variety of flours for baking and breading.** Coconut flour, garbanzo bean flower, almond flour, and buckwheat flower can be used in place of refined, white flour in most recipes.

**Variety of "good" grains.** Examples are whole grain brown rice, organic corn or organic rice pastas, soba noodles, quinoa, and grits. If you are gluten-free, stay away from whole wheat pastas and opt for gluten-free pasta (such as pastas made from rice or 100% buckwheat).

**All-natural nut butters.** Check the label and make sure that there are no sugars, hydrogenated oils, or preservatives added.

**Assortment of beans and legumes, dried and canned.** If using canned, check labels for additional ingredients added, and rinse before using.

**Assortment of vinegar flavors.** Experiment with these. They can be a wonderful way to add flavor, without added sugars, preservatives or calories. After all, vinegar is a natural preservative. Organic, raw apple cider vinegar is best. It can help alkalize your body, and it gives you a good source of probiotics. Use other vinegars such as balsamic, red wine, and white vinegar sparingly.

**Raw, local, organic honey.** Use honey in small amounts. No more than one tablespoon a day.

**Organic eggs, if you eat eggs.**

**Coconut milk, almond milk and plant-based milks.** Make sure they are the unsweetened varieties. You probably want to stay away from soy. The majority of soy in the U.S. is genetically modified, hard to digest, and likely to cause allergic reactions.

**Assortment of dried herbs and spices.** Stay away from most blends. Again, check the label and avoid the ones with undesired added ingredients. Organic only.

**Assortment of individual frozen vegetables.** These are great for quick meals and also great add-ins for soups and stews. Frozen peas and frozen butternut squash are great thrown into a soup for extra flavor and vitamins.

**Stevia.** This can be used in place of sugar. Stevia comes in packets, bulk, and liquid. Check the label for substitution instructions.

**Raw nuts and seeds.**

## Must-NOT-Haves

**Sugar.**

**Refined white flour.**

**Anything made from white flour.** Pasta, breads, baked goods, etc.

**Artificial sweeteners.**

**Agave nectar.** There is a lot of misinformation about agave nectar being a natural sweetener. It is actually processed, with more fructose than high fructose corn syrup! Run away from this substance!

**White rice.**

**Processed foods.** Processed foods are basically commercially prepared foods designed for ease of consumption. Examples are ready-to-eat foods, frozen meals, frozen pizzas, shelf-stable products, prepared mixes (such as cake mix), candies, sodas, and potato chips.

**Premade condiments, dressings and marinades.** Most of these have sugar and other unpronounceable ingredients.

**Sweetened fruit juices.**

**Anything containing trans fats.**

**High fat content or processed meat products.**

# The Ideal Diet

So now let's talk about what you CAN eat. The good news is there are at least 120,000 foods available after you start avoiding the Seven Deadly Sins.

Personally speaking, I have not consumed any animal products in over 30 years. I'm okay. Well, it depends on who you ask. ☺

I have never missed a meal because of my dietary choices. I've chosen to miss meals for certain reasons, but I've never missed a meal in a restaurant. I've never missed a meal on a cruise ship. I've never missed a meal at a resort. I've never been anywhere where I couldn't eat something.

When you put alcohol, meat, sugar, dairy, coffee, soda, and artificial sweeteners in your body, you stimulate the parts of your brain that get you high, and so you like them. And as weight-loss studies show, the four foods that stimulate your opiate receptor sites are meat, sugars, dairies, and chocolates.

If you are like many of us, you feel like you have absolutely no will-power when it comes to food. So I'm not asking you to give up all the Seven Deadly Sins at one time. I think that would be setting you up for failure. I'm just hoping that I've touched on a little bit of logic and common sense in your brain and that as you have been reading, you've thought, "That makes sense. I can see that." That's what I'm waiting for. The "that makes sense" part. Now how can we incorporate this into regular life?

## The SAD (standard American diet) Day

If you are the average person, a typical day starts with a cup of coffee and a breakfast food. Perhaps you lean toward a cheese Danish, cereal with milk, toast with jelly and butter, or a toaster pastry.

You go about your day and by midmorning, you are tired and starting to get hungry. You reach for a doughnut, cookie, or another simple sugar, and maybe another cup of coffee. Now you are watching the clock for lunchtime. Lunch is a sandwich of some sort, perhaps a burger on white bread. Maybe dinner includes pasta or pizza and a soda. In the next two hours, amazingly enough, you'll find your-self struggling to keep your eyes open and counting the minutes to bedtime so you can finally get some rest.

The next morning, you start all over again. Never once have you ever thought that, perhaps, what you are eating is one of the main reasons you are so tired all the time.

## The Ideal Diet Day

Now let me explain what a day looks like on the ideal diet, and then you can decide what works best for you.

In the morning, you wake up and drink 24 ounces of water with two tablespoons of raw, organic apple cider vinegar. Ideally, you'll prepare the water and vinegar before bed and place it on your nightstand for convenience. That water is going to help you do what? Pee, potty, tinkle—just pick your favorite euphemism.

Then you're going to get out of bed. You're going to walk to the bathroom. While you're walking, you're going to do some cross crawls (see chapter 8 for details) to stimulate your brain. Do your cross crawls on the way to the bathroom. They're easy, and you see the neurological effects on your body immediately. How cool is that?

What does a good day mean in terms of food?

**Breakfast.** The body is waking up. We're breaking a fast. That's where the word came from. If you've ever fasted, you know you want to come off a fast easy. You don't go on a six-day fast then have steak and potatoes for dinner. You have to introduce food again slowly so your body doesn't freak out. So fruit is the ideal way to start your day and break your fast. What kind of fruit?

- Apples
- Peaches
- Pears
- Bananas
- Pineapples

- Mangoes
- Kiwi
- Star fruit
- Watermelon
- Actually, any fruit will do

**Midmorning.** Now what's going to happen in a couple of hours? You're going to get hungry. Okay? I usually tell people to have their fruit, wait a couple of hours, and then eat something that's high in protein, high in fiber, and high in essential fatty acids, which is going to help your brain work and make you feel great. (See the section on omega oils in chapter 8.)

Then you have several options for your midmorning snack. A good one would be nuts and seeds like almonds, walnuts, pecans—anything except peanuts. Walnuts are high in omega-3 fatty acids. So, they would be a good choice, but any nut or seed will do.

Make sure they are raw nuts because the nutrients have been destroyed in roasted nuts. Now I want you to have two handfuls of nuts and stop, because if you're like me, you're going to want to eat more than that. That's going to hold you over till lunch.

## Recipes for the Health of It

If you want to learn how to make your own nondairy milk, receive a ton of information on how to change your diet, and find over 200 recipes, get a copy of my book *Eating Right . . . For the Health of It.*

Another option would be flaxseed "cereal." Flaxseed is high in the ever-vital omega-3 fatty acids. Take one tablespoon of whole flaxseed for every 50 pounds you weigh (you can go a little over if you want) and grind it in that coffee grinder you're not using for coffee anymore.

I usually add some raisins to the flaxseed (if you haven't had your maximum fruit allowance for the day), and maybe some dried coconut. Then I'll use a nondairy milk. You can make your own nut-based milk, but I'm going to be honest with you. I'm lazy, so I usually just buy it. And I have that as a little snack. If you want to get crazy with this, use ½ part flax seeds to ½ part hemp and/or chia seeds and grind them up. I know this may be living on the edge for some of you, so watch your excitement levels to make sure you don't overdo it!

In addition to being high in omega-3 fatty acids, flaxseed "cereal" is high in soluble and insoluble fiber. Soluble fiber is kind of slimy—like what you eat in oatmeal. There's a lot of soluble fiber in there. Soluble fiber is vital because when it gets in your digestive system, it's like the magnet that wraps itself around bad things, such as excess hormones and excess cholesterol. Oatmeal is great for that, as are flaxseeds, which also have insoluble fiber. This kind of fiber acts like a brush and pushes everything through the colon. Flaxseed cereal makes a great snack. It'll hold you over till lunch.

# Delayed Reaction

Here's another fun fact and a secret to weight loss. It takes 20 minutes to get a message from your tummy to your brain. You could eat for 20 minutes and feel full or you could eat two handfuls of nuts and wait 20 minutes to feel full. But it'll take 20 minutes either way for you to feel full. So get away from the food, because if it's there, you're going to eat it. I would. So, have two handfuls and get away from all other food.

**Lunch and dinner.** Now, for your lunch and dinner selections. Your choices are anything that isn't alcohol, meat, sugar, dairy, coffee, soda, or anything with artificial sweeteners. That narrows it down to about 120,000 choices.

You like Mexican food? How about a bean burrito instead of a beef burrito? Or a bean taco instead of a beef taco? Or fajitas without meat? How about guacamole? For bonus points, get a burrito in a bowl instead of a wrap and be sure to ask for no cheese or sour cream.

How about Chinese food? Stir-fried veggies? Kung Pao chicken? Get the Kung Pao vegetables without the meat.

My patients who start living and eating the way I recommend always think they must eat only salads when they go out to lunch or dinner. Salads are great, but I'm just trying to show that you truly do have many, many options out there that won't make you feel like you're miserable and you've given up EVERYTHING you enjoy in life.

So just look for things on the menu that don't have alcohol, meat, sugar, dairy, coffee, soda, or artificial sweeteners in them. There's always something on the menu. If you want to find it quickly, cover up the food and look at the prices. The healthy foods are always the cheapest thing on the menu. You win all the way around!

## A Challenge

You're drinking your eight glasses of water a day. You're doing your cross crawls for 30 seconds three times a day. You're trying to stay away from alcohol, meat, sugar, dairy, coffee, soda, and artificial sweeteners and to eat more fruits, vegetables, grains, nuts, and seeds.

Take this challenge and see what happens.

Eat, drink, and exercise the way I've described religiously for two weeks. At the end of two weeks, go ahead and have a nice big steak with cheese on it, yellow cheese, processed cheese food spread, and white bread with margarine and hydrogenated oil, because your liver needs something to do. Oh, and have a margarita while you're at it. And then see how you feel.

I can promise that you'll feel awful!

Then you can decide: "Do I want to feel awful all the time or feel good all the time?"

# Finding Umami Love

Whenever you order Chinese food, always make sure you get it with no MSG and no chicken broth. Chicken broth usually contains MSG, and the sauces often have MSG in them too, even when a restaurant declares no "added MSG." Side effects of MSG include headaches, blurred vision, dizziness, fatigue, digestive distress, and increased hunger.

Thai food often contains "fish sauce," a sauce made with fermented fish, which gives the dish that "Thai flavor." However, fish sauce usually contains MSG.

Some restaurants and chefs use MSG because it stimulates a recently discovered taste receptor. Yes, we actually found a new taste receptor in the human tongue! This taste receptor detects umami. Umami is a savory flavor (brothy, meaty) and produces a long-lasting, mouthwatering coating over the tongue. In the past, we always thought we had the taste receptors of sweet, salty, sour, and bitter. Umami is the flavor of foods that your taste receptors detect as not salty, sweet, sour, or bitter. The glutamic acid in MSG enhances the umami flavor and gives it that savory flavor.

Originally, MSG came from seaweed and didn't contain the concentrated glutamic acid that it contains today. Now we get MSG from bacteria, and the concentrated glutamic acid acts as an excitotoxin when it gets into the brain. An excitotoxin causes the brain to "fire faster" than it's supposed to and can actually burn out your brain cells. So, we're using a "flavor enhancer" that makes you want to eat more of that food but, in the long run, is horrible for the health of your brain.

I've been eating this way for several decades. I miss a meatball sandwich every now and then. Yeah, a Philly cheesesteak or sausage now and then. I miss it. I have to be honest.

But knowing what I now know, the reward of a tasty sandwich is not worth the risk. It's not worth it to me to take that chance. It just doesn't make any sense.

I know a lot of folks who stop drinking as they age. They tell me, "I have a couple of drinks, I feel bad for a couple of days afterward. It's not worth the tradeoff."

For me, indulging in the Seven Deadly Sins is not worth the tradeoff. I'd rather skip some food selections and feel great. Like my friends who have given up alcohol, it's just not worth the tradeoff of feeling awful.

But this is a decision you have to make for yourself—even though I can guarantee you'll never regret the decision once you've made it. It's interesting how many people tell me that they never realized how bad they felt until they changed their diet.

If you knew what I know, you'd do what I do.

# Cleanliness Is Next to Extreme Healthiness

Whenever I ask my patients if they cleanse and detoxify their bodies, they generally look at me as if I have three heads.

The standard American diet does not address the issue of cleansing and detoxifying our systems; it only adds to the problem. Most of us spend no time thinking about what toxic deposits are in our bodies.

I get asked quite frequently, "If I eat a perfect diet, should I have to detoxify?" The answer is *yes*, because it's not just diet that affects our body's toxicity.

We're exposed to car emissions, which could be high in mercury and toxic chemicals. We're exposed to perfumes, air fresheners, cleaning supplies, hair sprays, and things you may not keep in your environment, but you're exposed to because other people do. Did you ever walk into someone's home that was so filled with potpourri, candles, scented oils, and other air scents that it literally made you sick?

Most commercial potpourri, candles, air fresheners, scented oils, and perfumes contain chemicals that can disrupt your hormones. Ironically, lighting candles and putting on perfume for a romantic evening can actually increase your estrogen levels, thus effectively counteracting your testosterone levels, which are your "romantic hormones." Trying to make you and your house "smell pretty" can actually take the wind out of your sails when it comes to romance—and lead to other serious health issues by disrupting your hormones.

Air pollution and electromagnetic frequencies are other examples of toxic elements that get into our system. Remember all the fuss about cell phones causing brain cancer? I believe it's true. But every single day, millions of Americans walk around with their cell phones glued to their heads or their hands. A simple fix for this is to use a wired headset.

Add in stress and too little sleep, which can also severely harm your body, and you've got the perfect storm, even if you eat the perfect diet.

So cleansing and detoxifying really should be something you do periodically. It should just be part of your lifestyle. If you're putting good foods in, the body functions better, and it's able to eliminate the waste products. If you're putting bad foods in, the body can't eliminate as well as it should, and it could build up these toxins in the cells. So if you don't have a good diet, it's even more important that you cleanse and detoxify regularly.

## What's Normal Anyway?

What is normal when it comes to body detoxification? If you were ever a baby (and we all were at some point) or have taken care of a baby, you remember babies will eat and then poop. How did this baby end up making so much poo by eating so little food? Well, their body is working at maximum efficiency.

Think about it: food in should be food out. So if you're eating, you should be having a bowel movement at least twice a day. The best normal bowel function equals normal bowel movements twice a day—quick, easy, and clean. If you have excessive bowel function, it could be diarrhea. If you have fewer than two per day, it could be constipation.

Essentially, three different things can cause improper bowel activity: (1) the nerve supply to the bowels could be malfunctioning; (2) the bowels themselves could be having spasms and not working properly; and/or (3) your diet could be causing problems.

If you're eating a very good diet of mostly fruits, vegetables, nuts, and seeds; drinking a lot of water; and getting a lot of exercise, and your bowels still aren't working properly, then either your nerves or your bowels are causing the problems.

When this happens in my patients, I check their spines, making sure the nerves are working. The stomach pushing up against your diaphragm could also cause improper bowel function, which we discussed in chapter 3.

There's also a valve between your small and large intestine in the bottom right quadrant of your abdomen. If you draw a line between your belly button and the middle of your right hipbone, you'll discover the ileocecal valve. Sometimes that valve doesn't open and close like it's supposed to. If it's not opening properly, you can have constipation. If it's not closing properly, you can have diarrhea. Many times, I have to adjust that area in my patients to try to get the valve working properly again. Amazing how such a small thing can cause so much trouble, isn't it?

# Bad Breath and Your Digestive System

Bad breath can be another indication that folks need to "clean themselves out." Many people have chronic bad breath, which can be caused by rotten teeth or improper brushing and flossing. But bad breath can also come from improper bowel function. If breath smells like a bad bowel, it's usually coming from the digestive system.

(I think this is a good place for you to go, "EEEW!")

When food isn't being passed out properly, it rots in the colon. Gas coming from the rotting food gets absorbed into the blood system, which passes through your lungs, and then that smell is passed out in your breath.

So you can brush your teeth until the enamel comes off, but digestive problems can still cause bad breath.

You can take laxatives and stimulants to get your bowels moving, but you will just be treating the symptoms, not the cause. Sometimes it's okay to jump-start the bowels, but you have to make sure that your nervous system and your diet is working for your digestive system, not against it.

That's why I like my patients to "do some internal housecleaning." When the digestive system is working properly and you make sure you have no spasms or malfunction of the bowel muscles, you know that the controls (the nerves to the bowels) are working.

## Clear and Transparent

I know this isn't really "cocktail party" conversation. However, these things need to be said and explained clearly so you can make sure your body is working properly.

When you pee, it should be clear. As I said in chapter 2, you should be able to read the newspaper through the liquid. It should be that clear. But please don't try this at home and make a mess. I don't want your spouse or roommate calling and yelling at me. Vitamin B supplements can make your urine bright yellow, but it should still be clear. And it shouldn't have an odor to it or have particles floating in it.

Pee into a clear glass, cup, or jar and take a good look. If it's cloudy or has particles, there could be issues. If there's blood in the urine, that could be an issue as well.

From examining the urine, we can get a good idea of whether the kidneys and bladder are working properly. If not, we need to check the nervous system and your diet. You must make sure you're eating the right diet and drinking enough water—pure water.

## Water—Again

We've discussed water multiple times in this book already. But I want to tell you again how important it is to "detoxify" the water you drink. I personally believe that distilled water is best, but I admit that it's not very practical. At the very least, you should get a filter. You can get one in big box or home supply stores.

A filter you can put under your kitchen sink should work very well for your everyday use and be very practical. You'll have a source of pure water for drinking, cooking, and washing your fruits and veggies. We have home water filters available on our website, www.drjoeesposito.com.

If you don't want to go that far, at the very, very least, filter your water with something like a faucet filter or a tabletop pitcher filter. Tap water can have a lot of chlorine and fluoride and things you wouldn't expect—like drugs.

When people take drugs—legally or illegally—they can excrete traces of those drugs in their urine and feces. We eventually recycle this water but don't have sophisticated systems in place to filter out the drugs. Yuck. Think about it. If you don't filter your water, you are bathing in this stuff, cooking with it, drinking it, and watering your lawn with it. No wonder our bodies are so messed up.

You can go all the way through the whole house with filters for your water. They can be very expensive, but if you can afford it, I recommend a complete whole-house filter. This way, you're protecting yourself from all of the unwanted garbage that's in the American water system.

But if you can't go to that length, just figure out a way to filter your water as much as you can. My take is "any filter is better than no filter." No matter which filter you end up with, just be sure to keep up with the instructions on when it is time to change the filter.

# Your Deadly Morning Rituals

If you are like most of us, you start your morning by heading to your bathroom to get ready to face the day. But I bet you didn't know your daily rituals could be hurting your health and your family's health.

The soaps, lotions, creams, toothpaste, deodorants, sprays, shampoos, and even the laundry soaps you use on your towels might be the reasons you have less than perfect health.

## Protection Is Not Skin-Deep

Drinking water with chemicals in it is bad, but showering and bathing can also be bad for you if you're using water with chemicals in it. Your skin is a sponge, and things that come in contact with it can be absorbed through your skin and into your blood system. Your skin is a two-way street. Sweat and toxins can come out of your body through your skin, but toxins can also be absorbed into your skin. The skin can also let beneficial substances into your body. For example, instead of using lotions or soaps that contain hormone-disrupting chemicals, switch to extra-virgin organic coconut oil and castile soap. Coconut oil is good for the surface of your skin and is also good when it gets absorbed. Castile soap is made with natural oils and won't dry out your skin like many commercial soaps.

The outer layer of your skin—the epidermis—includes a lot of mature and dead cells. This layer is replaced about once every five weeks. The inner layer is called the dermis, and this layer is loaded with blood vessels and your lymphatic vessels. When a chemical or other substance gets down to this level, it can easily be absorbed into the blood and circulated throughout your body. Your skin is the largest organ in your body, weighing about 6 pounds and covering about 20 square feet in the average person.

The steam from your shower opens up your pores and dilates your lungs, giving chlorine and other chemicals two easy ways to enter your body. You can absorb as much chlorine through your open pores in a 15-minute hot shower as you do from drinking a glass of regular tap water. When you're in a hot shower, chlorine can also be absorbed through your lungs when you inhale the steam.

If you're not convinced I'm telling you the truth, try this. Pick up a swimming pool chlorine test kit. Fill a glass with your local tap water and test to see how much chlorine is in it. Now fill another glass from the same tap. Soak your hand in that glass for 60 seconds. Take your hand out and test for chlorine again. The water you just soaked your hand in will contain substantially less—or even no—chlorine: you absorbed the chlorine right into your skin. This is why I strongly recommend water filters for your kitchen sink and shower—although ideally, you would have a water filter for your entire house so that even the water in your toilets can't leak chlorine gas as the water evaporates as it sits in the toilet.

Chlorine is used in swimming pools and other water supplies to kill bacteria. But our bodies need much of our bacteria supply. Bacteria help digest our food, protect our skin from outside invaders, keep our immune system functioning properly, and play many other important roles in our bodily functions. Exposing ourselves to chlorine can destroy many good bacteria, and the adverse effects on our health can be far-reaching.

Women using tampons or pads are also frequently exposing themselves to chlorine because these products are usually bleached, and bleach contains—you guessed it—chlorine. I recommend you use feminine hygiene products that don't contain chlorine and other chemicals. Look in your local health food store for those products.

## Shaving

So let's continue examining your daily rituals.

If you shave, you probably start by putting some hot water on your skin to soften the whiskers or the hair on your legs, and then you apply shaving cream. The shaving cream lathers up, which we think is a good thing. However, most commercial shaving creams are loaded with toxic chemicals.

One of the very bad chemicals in most shaving creams is sodium lauryl sulfate. This ingredient is also found in most soaps and creams to help them foam up. It can cause skin irritation, dry skin, and cause vision problems if it gets in the eyes or is absorbed into the skin. If you use hot water when shaving, the hot water will open up the pores of your skin and give the chemicals an open route into your body. Sodium lauryl sulfate exposure can also lead to headaches, difficulty breathing, and hair loss. And if you cut yourself shaving, the chemicals have a clear path directly into your bloodstream.

## Toothpaste

After you shave and shower, you proceed to brush your teeth. If you ever take the time to read the side of a commercial tube of toothpaste, you will see a warning, something to the effect of: "Warning, harmful if swallowing more than amount used to normally brush teeth. If swallowed, call poison control." *Wait; what?*

There are chemicals in toothpaste that are harmful if swallowed, specifically fluoride, sodium lauryl sulfate, dyes, and—horror of all horrors—artificial sweeteners. The type of fluoride used in toothpaste, sodium fluoride, is in the same group of chemicals as arsenic and cyanide and can affect brain function. I have seen children who can focus better in school after they stop using toothpaste with this kind of fluoride.

Fluoride has also been linked to bone and oral cancers. If that isn't bad enough, a slick manufacturing trick is to make the toothpaste better by using artificial sweeteners such as aspartame or saccharine. You already know how I feel about that!

## Deodorant

Now that I have completely grossed you out by talking about bowels and pee and drugs in our water and scared you to death by describing the toxic chemicals in your morning rituals, let's move on to another "delicate" topic: armpit smell.

Now, let me say right up front—it's normal to sweat under your arms. However, if your armpit smell makes people move their seats away from you, you might need to give some thought to this section.

In the morning, you most likely put on an antiperspirant that contains aluminum. Some research has shown there may be links between aluminum buildup in the brain and Alzheimer's disease and other neurological conditions. Aluminum is a factor in speeding up the rate of brain aging. As noted on ScienceDirect.com, "Such acceleration would inevitably enlarge the incidence of age-related neurological diseases." Aluminum clogs our pores and prevents us from sweating, which is one way our body rids itself of toxins. The fragrance in anti-perspirants can cause allergic reactions and irritate your skin.

The good news is there are safe alternative products that work just as well, and in many cases better, than the products most likely sitting in your medicine cabinet today.

# Hairy Hideouts

If you want to cut down on your use of deodorant, try shaving your armpits. That will cut down on the armpit smell that causes you to reach for deodorant in the first place.

Why? Bacteria can live in the hair in your armpits. Their existence in your "armpit hair condo" can create an unpleasant smell.

## *Alternatives*

There are also safer products available in health food stores or online that you can substitute for your shaving creams and soaps and deodorants. The nontoxic shave creams may not foam up as well as commercial shave creams, but they do a better job at removing whiskers without drying out your skin.

You can also use castile soap, not only to clean your body, but as a shave cream. Castile soap is made with plant oils and removes most dirt as well as commercial soap. It is so safe, you can even eat it—although I wouldn't really recommend that.

If something is going to be absorbed into your skin, you want to make sure it will not make you sick. So choose wisely.

There are several toothpastes available that do not have fluoride, artificial sweeteners, or sodium lauryl sulfate. Use deodorant instead of antiperspirant, and only use ones that do not contain aluminum.

You might have to try a few different brands to find one that works for you, but it is worth it to protect your health.

If you want to make your own natural deodorant, combine 3 ounces of rubbing alcohol and 1 ounce water; then mix in about 15 to 20 drops of natural/essential tea tree oil. You can safely spray that concoction under your arms. This recipe works very well, but its effects don't always last throughout the day. So you may have to put some on in the morning and reapply at lunch. A bit of a pain, but it's definitely a more natural way to fight underarm odor.

Another easy recipe is to combine 1 part baking soda, 1 part pure shea butter, 1 part organic coconut oil, and a few drops of tea tree oil or your favorite essential oil. Heat the shea butter briefly in a double boiler to soften it before you combine it with the other ingredients. Store in a covered glass jar. Apply a tiny bit under your arms with your fingertips.

You can purchase laundry detergents and dishwashing soaps that contain no toxic chemicals; as a bonus, these products are also usually hypoallergenic. They work very well and are just as easy to use as their commercial counterparts. Many times I have seen patients with unexplained rashes, allergies, and fatigue respond very well when they switch to a more natural laundry soap.

Making some simple changes in your usual personal hygiene products might be preventing health problems, not only now, but also in the future.

# Clearing the Buildup

Regular cleansing, fasting, and other detoxifying programs help the body rid itself of built-up toxins. Even a person on a perfectly healthy diet will accumulate waste materials over time, not to mention the buildup of chemicals from our air, water and food.

## How Do You Detoxify?

The best way to achieve colon cleansing is by eating a good diet of fruits, vegetables, grains, nuts, and seeds, making sure about 80 percent of that is raw, and consuming plenty of flaxseed and other fibers. However, if you need a jump-start, you might want to try Dr. Joe's Intestinal Cleanser.

Here's the story behind this product. Several years ago, a 16-year-old girl came to me with constipation problems. She was only having two to three bowel movements a month. Yes, you read it right, two to three a *month*. Obviously, this was a very serious issue, and her parents had spent a lot of money to find out what was going on.

Their last hope—after me—was to travel to Cincinnati for a special test to see if her colon was actually contracting. If not, they would put her on a special medication. I asked her parents, "Why don't we just put her on the medication to see if it works?" I didn't know why they should keep this poor girl in misery and spend $10,000 on a test.

But they weren't keen on putting her on the medication, so I told them I would try to get to the root of the problem. We got her under chiropractic care and got her diet straightened out. She went from having two to three bowel movements a month to two to three bowel movements a week. No medication.

Better. But still not ideal.

So I created Dr. Joe's Intestinal Cleanser. It worked great for her. She took it daily for a few months. In that time her colon returned to normal function. It's a herbal pill that works extremely well to jump-start the bowels. This product is NOT for someone who experiences frequent diarrhea—only for someone who experiences frequent constipation.

In this case, we're treating the symptom, but sometimes we need to treat the symptom in order to get the body working normally again. Then we can work on the root cause.

If you DO take Dr. Joe's Intestinal Cleanser, I recommend that you take only one pill, at night. See how you do during the night and the next day. If your bowels are moving two to three times the next day, that's all you need. If they still aren't moving, you might want to take two pills. The next day, if they still aren't moving, you can increase to three pills.

Don't take more than three!

Trust me on this one. I had a patient who took six pills at once. Her exact words to me were, "Dr. Joe, that stuff REALLLLLLLLLY works!"

The goal with the intestinal cleanser is get the bowels moving so that you can stop taking the cleanser. By discontinuing use, it will give you time to ensure the body is functioning normally again, that the nervous system is working, that the muscles and the bowels are working, and that you have a good diet.

## Sleep

Another way your body detoxifies itself is through sleep. When you sleep, your body cleanses itself and gets rid of junk. That's why, when you wake up after a good night's rest, your hair and skin are greasy, your breath stinks, your armpits smell. You get the picture.

During sleep, your body cleans out all of the junk. If you're not sleeping properly, you're not going through this cleansing and detoxifying phase.

Now, think about this—you can be awake for eight hours and your hair or skin won't be greasy, your armpits won't stink. But if you sleep for eight hours, you stink! That's proof that your body is cleansing itself during sleep.

A neat way to tell how toxic you are is to take a metal spoon and scrape your tongue when you first wake up in the morning. Scrape it back to front, covering your whole tongue. If you get a lot of white, goopy, mucous-y, yellow-y stuff, that's a sign that your body is doing a lot of work to detoxify.

As you get your body and diet straightened out, you can scrape your tongue again and see that you're getting less and less of the icky stuff. It's a good way to monitor your toxification level and monitor your progress in lowering that level.

# Reboot Your Body with R&R

Giving your body an opportunity to restore itself must be a priority if you want to be healthy. This includes learning the proper sleeping posture, having regular sleep times, practicing meditation and relaxation techniques. And having lots of fun!

## Dr. Joe's Sleeping Recommendations

In chapter 10, we talked about how a good night's sleep can help cleanse your body of toxins. Sleep offers other benefits to your health too. In order to make sure you can get the kind of sleep that will be most beneficial to your body, you need to follow a couple of rules.

- Follow a regular sleep schedule. Now, sometimes this is not possible, but our bodies do have something called circadian rhythms, which are designed to help the body sleep when it's dark and wake up when it's light. That's the ideal.

- When you go to sleep, make sure your room is as dark as possible. Use blackout curtains, sleep masks, etc.

- If you have lights in your room—clock radios, TVs, etc.—cover them. Why is this so important? When it gets dark, your brain starts producing melatonin. As soon as light comes through your eyelids, melatonin production can be altered.

- Sleep in a quiet area. If this isn't possible, get yourself some earplugs.

- You can utilize ambient or "white noise" in your sleeping area. You can even get phone apps that will play these types of sounds while you sleep, but be mindful of the light emitting from your phone. As a general rule, quiet is always the ideal.

- Set the temperature of your room at 65 to 70 degrees Fahrenheit.

## Sleep and Diet

If you're not sleeping properly, you need to get your digestion checked. If your digestive system isn't working properly, you may not be able to produce the chemicals you need to help you sleep.

Your stomach breaks down proteins into amino acids. The amino acid tryptophan gets into your small intestine and provides the vitamin B6 chemical called 5HTP, which becomes serotonin, which becomes melatonin.

If you can't sleep, your body may not be making enough melatonin. This can cause you to be anxious and mentally unsettled—all because your digestive system isn't working properly.

If you frequently find yourself getting up in the middle of the night to make a trip to the potty, you should limit fluid intake after 3 p.m.

If you're young, this is probably not an issue for you. However, as you age, it is harder for your body to hold your urine, and so it wakes you up in the middle of the night. You may need to apply the same time restrictions to "watery foods," such as watermelon or salads.

## Troubling Midnight Runs

Midnight bathroom trips can be real problems for men with prostate issues. So we want to get to the cause of the prostate issues. If you are a man and are having to go to the bathroom a lot during the night even AFTER you have limited your fluid intake, you are going to want to get this problem checked out.

Before you go to bed, you should eat light because digestion can be very stimulating to the body. It takes a lot of energy. You should especially stay away from acidic foods, which can also be very stimulating. Again, we're back to the Seven Deadly Sins. Just in case you've forgotten, these are alcohol, meat, sugars, dairy, coffee, sodas, and artificial sweeteners.

You should really try to eat alkaline foods such as vegetables and salads (but be careful of the fluid content) late in the day. The lighter you eat before bed, the better you're going to feel.

You should stop eating about three or four hours before you go to sleep. These last hours before bedtime should be spent relaxing and unwinding, not getting stressed out, working, or doing paperwork. This should be your downtime. Your body needs downtime.

If you do drink caffeine or alcohol before bed, remember, it doesn't give you energy, it merely blocks the adenosine receptor sites that make you feel less tired, as we discussed earlier in the book. You may not think that the caffeine is keeping you awake, but bear in mind that it may be preventing you from getting into the deepest sleep possible. A lot of people do drink caffeine and alcohol before they go to bed, but it can definitely affect the depth of sleep that you experience, which your body desperately needs.

# Dr. Joe's Meditation and Relaxation Techniques

Overdoing anything can and usually does lead to burn-out, which makes you less productive. Remember, this life is not a dress rehearsal; if you are enjoying what you do and could not imagine doing anything else, then keep doing it! If not, take time out to enjoy life. From what I understand, no one on their deathbed ever said, "I should have spent more time in the office, on my computer and less time playing and having fun."

One way to deal with stress is to practice deep breathing exercises. When we get stressed, we tend to hold our breath. Try taking a real deep breath, breathing in for a slow count of 5, holding the breath for a slow count of 15, and exhaling for a slow count of 5. Be sure to exhale all your breath. Do this 10 times and watch how much better you feel.

You may suffer from negative emotions toward a friend, family member, or loved one. You must purge yourself of anger and hatred in order to boost your immune system.

You can help keep your immune system happy by adopting the mind-set of believing in yourself, being good to yourself, expectantly waiting for good things to happen to you, seeing the beauty all around you, and practicing a "seize the day" attitude. We only get one chance on this earth, so don't waste time with unimportant matters.

When you are stressed about something, consider if what is bothering you is worth damaging your health. Will this situation be important a year from now, or even a week from now? If not, don't stress over it.

It may not only be mental stress that weakens the system, but physical stress. Physical stress can be pain, pinched nerves, or sitting too long during the day. Even poorly fitting shoes can cause physical stress.

If you're lost and don't know what to do, consider taking yoga classes or meditation classes, and/or volunteering for a cause you believe in.

## Do What You Love

One of the leading risk factors for not surviving your first heart attack is job dissatisfaction!

Yes, you read that correctly! Not diet, not genetics, not medical treatment, but job dissatisfaction! Scary thought, boys and girls. In the past, we thought it was just a nice idea that you should spend time doing things you believe in and love to do. Now we know that it is critical to health and longevity. The healthiest people live life to the fullest!

Maybe your passion is cooking, reading, skiing, being with family, or just spending time alone. Right now, consider one or two things that make you smile just thinking about them. Then follow your passion and work those activities into your schedule.

*I know, I know, you don't have time.*

But I truly believe that you may not have the option of NOT putting them in your schedule.

Everyone needs time to decompress, relieve stress, and reconnect with the part of them that brings the most joy. This makes life more enjoyable, helps us to cope with the stressors of our lives, and gives us the positive physiological result of an endorphin rush. This endorphin rush gives us our feelings of joy, invincibility, and relaxation.

## My Momma Said

My mother told me, "I don't care if you are a garbage man, just be the best garbage man you can be." I've always tried to follow her advice, and I've tried to find ways to help other people follow this advice.

Incorporate these simple ideas to help you insert passion and purpose into your life and see what happens. There are tons of books and resources about this subject, but here's my simple advice: Do what you love. The money, the solutions, the resources will all come to your aid. When you decide to finally do what you love, it's as if the world says to you, "It's about time. Let's send him some clients, some contacts, some resources so he can finally get it in gear."

If you figure out why you are doing what you are doing (ideally, what you love), the "how" part (the logistical stuff like finding clients, money, and whatever else you need) will "magically" appear, right on time.

If I'm wrong, so what, nothing was lost. But if I'm right (and I am), you will see an amazing change for the better in all aspects of your life. You may find yourself with a new hobby, career, or complete new life!

# Conclusion

As you get older, you keep depleting your body of nutrients. It's like you were given a trust account from your dead uncle and you keep withdrawing from it. Every day you take a little money out, a little money out, a little money out. If you don't put any back in, eventually you will go bankrupt. I don't want you to become nutritionally bankrupt like so many Americans are today.

What happens when our "health account" is empty? We turn to emergency medicine:

- My pancreas isn't working. I've got to take drugs.
- I've got a lump in my breast. I've got to get a mastectomy.
- My gallbladder isn't working. I've got to get it removed.

"We don't got extra parts, guys," as my New Jersey boys would say. Our bodies aren't cars; we can't just go out and buy new parts. We only have what we have—and none of our parts are expendable, either.

Doctors used to believe that the appendix had no real function, but now we're finding out that it has a vital function. Research has shown that it helps prevent colon cancer.

So we pulled out millions of appendixes in earlier years. Can we put them back in? Can't do that. We don't have extra parts. And we're depleting the parts we have every day—with alcohol, meat, sugar, dairy, coffee, soda, and artificial sweeteners, and other such poisons. When we pour those poisons into our body, it cannot function at its peak performance.

Even though more money is spent on healthcare in America than in most other countries (for example, America spends 17.1 percent of the gross domestic product on healthcare versus a country like Australia, which spends 9.4 percent on healthcare), we don't seem to be getting any healthier. We spend the most on healthcare, and we're the sickest people. It's crazy.

My goal is to return to the common-sense approach to health: treat the cause, not the symptom. I'll say it again and again: I'm not against drugs or surgery; I'm just against using them to cover up symptoms that can be cured.

In order to obtain and maintain good health, you need to take control of your own healthcare. I want to help you get well and stay well.

I hope that you have discovered some practical principles in this book that you can carry with you for the rest of your life.

Whenever I educate my radio listeners, patients, or seminar attendees, I seem to hear the same comment made over and over: "Why didn't someone tell me these things sooner?"

That is why I've written this book. So that this message of hope and education can reach more people than I could reach through my practice, radio shows, and speeches. I want America and the world to return to the common-sense, practical principles that can get them well and keep them well.

You're probably already spending energy, money, and resources on healthcare every time you get sick. Why not use just half of those resources to stop yourself from getting sick?

You never know how something we think, do, or say today will affect the lives of millions tomorrow. I can only hope that what I have shared with you in this book can make a difference in your life—and help you make a positive difference in the lives of others around you.

Here's to your health!

# Dr. Joe's Secrets
## for Extreme Athletes

### Nutrition and Menu Planning

I
n my practice, I do run across the occasional marathon runner, tri-
athlete, bodybuilder, really seriously athletic weekend warrior, or just
a plain ol' gym rat, as they used to say back in the '80s. These extreme
athletes want to know if the diet and nutrition guidelines I've advo-
cated in this book can actually work for them. Yes! It just takes a little
more knowledge and specialized information. So, this section is for
those of you who will never need my advice on slipping a little exercise
into your routine.

You must develop lifelong good nutritional habits, whether you're
a serious athlete or just a faithful exerciser. Look at all the nutrition
information in this book, specifically the lists in chapter 9 about the
ingredients you should always have on hand in your kitchen—and the
ones you should *avoid* placing in your kitchen. But if you're really out
there burning up extreme amounts of calories in your workouts, you
need to know more about nutrition than the average reader. So read on
for some additional facts on nutritional components you need to know.

## Carbohydrates

Carbohydrates are essential to proper function of the brain, spinal cord,
nerves, and muscles. Your brain controls everything, and carbohydrates
are the primary fuel for brain function. Carbohydrates are converted to
glucose, which the body needs as fuel. Once the cells have enough glucose
to run efficiently, the excess carbohydrates are converted to glycogen,
to be stored so the body has a supply on hand when the glucose in the
cells is used up.

When the glycogen storage places (liver, muscles, etc.) are filled up,
the excess glycogen is sent to the liver, converted to triglycerides, and
eventually stored as fat. Understanding this process helps you see why
it's important to get the proper amount of carbohydrates to meet your

energy needs, but not leave too many out there to be turned into fat stores.

Brown rice, fruits, vegetables, beans, oats, millet, quinoa and root vegetables are all good sources of carbohydrates. Bad sources are sugar, wheat, white rice, and fruit juices.

These sources are not good because they convert to glucose very quickly; then the glucose is absorbed into your blood system, which will raise your insulin levels. The insulin will move the glucose out of your blood into the cells, which will give you a rush of energy. But this rush of insulin will take too much glucose out of your blood, which will all too soon lead to low blood sugar, which will decrease your performance and energy.

Gluten products can be a major enemy to an endurance athlete. Gluten causes excess mucus, which affects breathing and lung function and creates digestive issues. Athletes definitely don't want to experience either of those problems during an event!

Wheat, spelt, barley, and rye have gluten. These glutens contain gliadins, which are proteins that can irritate your intestines and prevent proper absorption of nutrients. Gluten can also cause mucus production in your digestive system, sinuses, and lungs. This can prevent proper oxygen utilization and have a very serious adverse effect on your athletic performance as well as your overall health.

**KNOW YOUR CARBS**

**Good Sources of Carbohydrates**

- Brown rice
- Fruits
- Vegetables
- Beans and legumes (such as lentils and peas)
- Oats
- Millet
- Quinoa
- Root vegetables (potatoes, parsnips, carrots, sweet onions, beets)

**Poor Sources of Carbohydrates**

- Sugar
- Wheat
- White rice
- Fruit juices

The key to getting the proper amount of carbohydrates is to consume high-fiber and complex carbohydrates that will be absorbed slowly and give you a steady release of glucose—better known as energy.

*Rules for Carbohydrate Consumption Before/During/After Workout*
Consume 50–100 grams of carbohydrates about 30 to 60 minutes before your workout. You could get your carbs by eating a couple of natural granola bars—the kind with no added chemicals or high fructose corn syrup—a potato, or about one cup of brown rice.

While you are heavily exercising, consume 30–70 grams of carbohydrates per hour. This could mean eating a piece of fruit, a serving of a root vegetable about the size of your hand, a natural granola bar, a handful of dried fruit such as raisins (be sure there are no sulfites in your dried fruit and always choose organic when possible) or a handful or two of trail mix (again, no sulfites).

**Good Sources of Proteins**

- Nuts
- Seeds
- Beans
- Legumes
- Plant-based milks such as rice, almond or hemp milk
- Organic eggs
- Gluten-free grains

# Protein

Protein is not a great source of fuel, but it is essential in building muscle mass. Most people get more than enough protein in their diets, so figuring out just the right amount of protein is important. Great sources of protein are nuts, seeds, beans, plant-based milks, such as unsweetened rice, almond, and hemp milk, organic eggs, and gluten-free grains.

If you are a meat eater, lean cuts of meat can be a great source of protein. Unfortunately, most meat products are loaded with additional chemicals and steroids. Try to eat organic, grass-fed meat, and limit meat consumption to two to three times a week.

As I said above, you need protein to build muscle mass, and most folks eat more than enough protein, but it is the quality of the protein we want to discuss.

Although dairy is a source of protein, like meat, it might be loaded with steroids, chemicals, hormones, and antibiotics. If you do consume dairy, make it organic. Like gluten, dairy causes excess mucous production that can inhibit your ability to intake and utilize oxygen, so it may be advisable to eliminate it altogether.

From Dr. Joe's point of view, just say no to dairy.

# Fat

Everyone has heard the phrase "good fats versus bad fats." But what does it mean exactly? The best sources of fats are nonprocessed and plant-based. Avoid hydrogenated oils, anything with trans fat, and most vegetable oils. Remember, oils high in omega-6 fatty acids can increase inflammation, slow healing, and increase pain—never good for athletes!

**KNOW YOUR FATS**

**Oils High in Omega-6 Fatty Acids (Not Good)**

- Peanut oil
- Safflower oil
- Corn oil
- Soy oil

**Good Sources of Fat**

Most of these good sources are high in omega-3 fatty acids, which help repair tissue damage, improve neurological function, and reduce inflammation.

- Nuts and nut butters, raw if possible
- Olive oil
- Ground flax seeds, ground hemp seeds, ground sesame seeds (about 2 tablespoons a day of either of these)
- Flax oil
- Avocados
- Chlorella and spirulina (plankton)
- Krill oil (if you eat animal products)

# Hydration for the Serious Athlete

Water is an important nutrient for any athlete. Athletes should be fully hydrated before the start of any event and should replace as much lost fluid as possible by drinking cool liquids at frequent intervals during the event. Cool fluids are absorbed faster and help lower body temperature. During an event, it is more beneficial to drink smaller quantities at frequent intervals than to drink larger amounts infrequently.

The day before an event, drink fluids frequently, but don't overhydrate. If you hear "sloshing" in your stomach, skip the next interval of water. Hydrate frequently the following day after your event. It may take up to 36 hours to completely rehydrate.

## *Hydration Recommendations for Athletic Events*

| Meal | Fluid Intake |
| --- | --- |
| Pre-event meal | 2–3 cups water |
| 2 hours before | 2–2 ½ cups water |
| ½ hour before | 2 cups water |
| Every 10–15 minutes during the event | ½ cup cool (45–55 degrees) water |
| After event | 2 cups fluid for each pound lost |
| Next day | Drink fluids frequently (may take 36 hours to rehydrate completely) |

# Dr. Joe's Nutrition Tips for the Serious Athlete

**Important note:** Don't make any dietary changes a week before a major athletic event. Your body will not have time to adjust to the changes, which could cause undesirable side effects and impact your performance.

Nutrition and performance go hand in hand, especially for the endurance athlete. What you eat, when you eat, and how much you eat can determine your level of success. Proper nutrition can help alleviate digestive issues, muscle fatigue, and joint damage, which many athletes face.

Determining the proper foods and timing of meals to optimize maximum performance and recovery can be tricky. This section is designed to provide basic information, tips, guidelines, and recipes to help every athlete achieve that taste of victory!

## Nutrition Points to Consider

Do not compromise your health in the name of athletic performance. A decision you make today to enhance your performance will have an impact on you the rest of your life.

You have to eat anyway; you might as well eat the proper foods that can provide optimum health and optimum performance.

You must have the proper amount of vitamins, minerals, carbohydrates, fats, proteins, water, and micronutrients on a regular basis to perform at your peak.

It's not just what you eat, it's also what you *don't* eat that will determine how well you perform and recover from an athletic event.

Listen to your body! Pain that does not lessen in three days, fatigue, brain fog, digestive problems, irregular or lack of menstrual cycles could be signs of a health issue that may require professional help.

Learn to read food labels. Many foods have added ingredients that you don't want in your body. Added sugar is a big culprit. If you can't pronounce an ingredient, don't eat it!

Just because a food is labeled "healthy," "gluten-free," "low carbohydrate," or "low fat" doesn't necessarily mean it is good for you. Many foods with these claims have undesired added ingredients to make them taste better. The fewer ingredients on a label, the better. Keep it simple!

## Recipes for Victory

It is possible to prepare a wide range of meals that meet your dietary requirements, taste delicious, and get you ready for a big event. And you don't have to be a master chef to prepare these recipes!

I'm giving you a variety of recipes that fit into many nutrition plan categories, such as gluten-free, vegan, vegetarian, paleo, primal, and wheat belly. If you need to increase the carbohydrate content on some of the lower-carb recipes, simply add an extra food item from the "good carbs" listed above. Many of the recipes offer substitutions or additions to modify them for your diet.

## Each Day for Three Days Prior to an Event

For average athletes weighing 175 pounds, it is recommended you consume 2,625 calories per day (approximately 15 calories per pound of body weight). To get those calories, you should take in 1,050 calories of carbohydrates, 1,050 calories of protein, and 525 calories of fat.

### Meal One

    3 organic eggs

    1/2 cup oatmeal

    1 cup soy, rice almond, or hemp milk

    3/4 teaspoon olive oil

### Meal Two

Smoothie with 1 banana, 2 tablespoons rice protein, 1 cup coconut, rice, almond or hemp milk, 2 tablespoons "green drink" (Dr. Joe's Super Greens or Essential Source)

### Meal Three

1 cup beans, peas, or lentils

1/2 baked organic potato (with skin)

1/2 cup raw broccoli

1/2 teaspoon of flaxseed oil

### Meal Four

Smoothie with 1 banana, 2 tablespoons rice protein, 1 cup coconut, rice, almond, or hemp milk, 2 tablespoons "green drink" (Dr. Joe's Super Greens or Essential Source)

### Meal Five

5 oz. tempeh (fermented soybean in a block)

3/4 cup brown rice

1/4 cup mixed vegetables

1/2 teaspoon flaxseed oil

### Meal Six

Smoothie with 1 banana, 2 tablespoons rice protein, 1 cup soy, rice, almond, or hemp milk, 2 tablespoons "green drink"

## The Pre-Event Meal

A pre-event meal three to four hours before the event allows for optimal digestion and energy supply. I recommend small pregame meals that provide 500 to 1,000 calories.

The meal should be high in starch, which breaks down more easily than protein and fats. The starch should be in the form of complex carbohydrates (beans, legumes, millet, quinoa, gluten-free pasta, brown or wild rice, fruits and vegetables). Starches are digested at a rate that provides consistent energy to the body and are emptied from the stomach in two to three hours.

High-fiber carbohydrates push food through your colon, giving you a slow release of sugar. High-sugar foods lead to a rapid rise in blood sugar, followed by a decline in blood sugar and less energy. In addition, concentrated sweets can draw fluid into the gastrointestinal tract and contribute to dehydration, cramping, nausea, and diarrhea.

Don't consume any carbohydrates one and a half to two hours after an event. This may lead to premature exhaustion of glycogen stores in endurance events.

Avoid a meal high in fats. Fat takes longer to digest and can clump your red blood cells together, preventing oxygen from getting to your muscles. Take in adequate fluids during this pregame time. Avoid caffeine (cola, coffee, tea), which may lead to dehydration by increasing urine production.

Don't ignore the psychological aspect of eating foods you enjoy and tolerate well before an event. However, choose wisely—if you eat meat, bake organic meat instead of frying it.

Some athletes may prefer a liquid pre-event meal. A liquid meal will move out of the stomach by the time a meet or match begins. Remember to include water with this meal!

Regardless of age, gender, or sport, the pre-event meal recommendations are the same.

## *Pre-Event Meal Suggestions*

### Meal Plan I (approximately 500 calories)
1 cup coconut, rice, hemp, or almond milk

2 oz. beans, nuts, or seeds

1 serving (1/2 cup) fruit

1 medium organic potato

1 tsp. fat spread such as olive oil, flaxseed, or hemp oil

### Meal Plan II (approximately 900 calories)
2 cups coconut, rice, hemp, or almond milk

2 oz. beans, nuts, or seeds

1 serving (1/2 cup) fruit

1 cup pasta (rice or corn would be best) or 1 medium baked potato

1 tsp. fat spread such as olive oil, flaxseed, or hemp oil

1 serving (1/2 cup) raw vegetables

Handful of organic dried fruit or 1 cup smoothie with no added sugar for dessert

## *Meals to Eat after an Event*

Following a training session or competition, a small meal eaten within 30 minutes is very beneficial. The meal should contain protein and fat. Protein synthesis is greatest during the window of time immediately following a workout.

It is important to replace the nutrients lost during an event. So try to eat at least one of these suggested foods at each meal for three days following an event. Most people are magnesium deficient after athletic events, and this will help replace the magnesium you need.

Magnesium is vital to prevent muscle spasms, thus allowing proper circulation and proper healing. The table below shows some healthy foods that are high in magnesium.

| Food Item | Serving Size | Magnesium (mg) |
|---|---|---|
| Black beans | 1 cup | 120 |
| Raw broccoli | 1 cup | 22 |
| Nuts | 1 ounce | 64 |
| Frozen okra | 1 cup | 94 |
| Raw plantain | 1 medium | 66 |
| Pumpkin and squash seeds | 1 ounce (142 seeds) | 151 |
| Cooked spinach | 1 cup | 157 |
| Organic tempeh | ¼ block | 37 |
| Whole grain cereal, ready to eat | ¾ cup | 24 |
| Whole grain cereal, cooked | 1 cup | 56 |
| Whole wheat bread | 1 slice | 4 |

Now, remember, that a pre-event meal or special diet for several days prior to competition cannot make up for an inadequate daily food intake in previous months or years.

By combining this bonus material along with the other information in this book, you are sure to feel the best you've ever felt in your life, while also being able to achieve your fitness goals!

# Works Cited

Agersø, Yvonne, Henrik Hasman, Lina M. Cavaco, Karl Pedersen, and Frank M. Aarestrup. 2012. "Study of Methicillin Resistant Staphylococcus Aureus (MRSA) in Danish Pigs at Slaughter and in Imported Retail Meat Reveals a Novel MRSA Type in Slaughter Pigs." *Veterinary Microbiology*, no. 1–2. Retrieved June 16, 2016.

Asprey, D. (1991). "Why Bad Coffee Makes You Weak." *Bulletproof: The State of High Performance*. www.bulletproofexec.com/why-bad-coffee-makes-you-weak/.

Barnard, Neal D., and Joanne Stepaniak. 2003. *Breaking the Food Seduction: The Hidden Reasons Behind Food Cravings—and 7 Steps to End Them Naturally*. New York: Macmillan.

Bondy, Stephen C. 2016. "Low Levels of Aluminum Can Lead to Behavioral and Morphological Changes Associated with Alzheimer's Disease and Age-Related Neurodegeneration." *Neurotoxicology* 52, January: 222–229. Retrieved June 28, 2016.

Bowers, Becky. "Rep. Louise Slaughter Says 80% of Antibiotics Are Fed to Livestock." *Politifact*. Last modified October 15, 2013. www.politifact.com/truth-o-meter/statements/2013/oct/15/louise-slaughter/rep-louise-slaughter-says-80-antibiotics-are-fed-l/#.

Chong, Daniel H. "Real or Synthetic: The Truth Behind Whole-Food Supplements." Mercola.com. Retrieved June 24, 2016. http://articles.mercola.com/sites/articles/archive/2005/01/19/whole-food-supplements.aspx.

Costa, Wellington Luis Reis, Jeane dos Santos Ferreira, Joelza Silva Carvalho, Ellayne Souza Cerqueira, Lucimara Cardoso Oliveira, and Rogeria Comastri de Castro Almeida. 2015. "Methicillin-Resistant Staphylococcus Aureus in Raw Meats and Prepared Foods in Public Hospitals in Salvador, Bahia, Brazil." *Journal of Food Science* 80, no. 1: M147–50. Retrieved June 16, 2016.

De la Monte, Suzanne M., and Jack R. Wands. 2008. "Alzheimer's Disease Is Type 3 Diabetes-Evidence Reviewed." *Journal of Diabetes Science and Technology* 2, no. 6: 1101–13. Retrieved June 17, 2016.

Donovan, Christine. 2015. "If FDA Does Not Regulate Food, Who Will? A Study of Hormones and Antibiotics in Meat Production." *American Journal of Law & Medicine* 459. Retrieved June 17, 2016.

Dragoni, S., J. Gee, R. Bennett, M. Valoti, and G. Sgaragli. 2006. "Red Wine Alcohol Promotes Quercetin Absorption and Directs Its Metabolism Towards Isorhamnetin and Tamarixetin in Rat Intestine *In Vitro*." *British Journal of Pharmacology* 147, no. 7: 765–71. http://dx.doi.org/10.1038/sj.bjp.0706662.

Environmental Working Group. "The Clean Fifteen." EWG.org. Retrieved June 27, 2016. www.ewg.org/foodnews/clean_fifteen_list.php.

———. "The Dirty Dozen." EWG.org. Retrieved June 27, 2016. www.ewg.org/foodnews/dirty_dozen_list.php.

Espat, A. May 2015. "Does Sugar Love Cancer?" MD Anderson Cancer Center. Retrieved January 1, 2016. www.mdanderson.org/patient-and-cancer-information/cancer-information/cancer-topics/prevention-and-screening/food/cancersugar.html.

Federation of American Societies for Experimental Biology. "Anti-Inflammatory Effects of Omega 3 Fatty Acid in Fish Oil Linked to Lowering of

Prostaglandin." *ScienceDaily.* Retrieved June 24, 2016. www.sciencedaily.com/releases/2006/04/060404085719.htm.

Fein, Alan. February 2012. "Nociceptors and the Perception of Pain." *University of Connecticut Health Center.* Retrieved June 30, 2016. http://cell.uchc.edu/pdf/fein/nociceptors_fein_2012.pdf.

Greger, Michael. "Why Are Chickens Fed Prozac?" Last modified January 26, 2016. http://nutritionfacts.org/2016/01/26/why-are-chickens-fed-prozac/.

Grygus, Andrew. "OILS CHART—Smoke Temperature, Composition & Stability." Clovegarden.com. Retrieved June 24, 2016. www.clovegarden.com/ingred/oilchart.html.

Hanson, B.M., A.E. Dressler, A.L. Harper, R.P. Scheibel, S.E. Wardyn, L.K. Roberts, J.S. Kroeger, and T.C. Smith. 2011. "Prevalence of Staphylococcus Aureus and Methicillin-Resistant Staphylococcus Aureus (MRSA) on Retail Meat in Iowa." *Journal of Infection and Public Health* 4, 169–74. Retrieved June 16, 2016.

"Harmful Effects of Excess Sugar." *Ask Dr. Sears.* Retrieved June 20, 2016. www.askdrsears.com/topics/feeding-eating/family-nutrition/sugar/harmful-effects-excess-sugar.

Levine, Beth. "Soda and Kidney Disease." Jonbarron.org. Last modified November 28, 2013. https://jonbarron.org/alternative-cancer/Preventing-Cancer-and-Diabetes-by-Not-Drinking-Sodas#.V2msc_krKHu.

Liou, Stephanie. "Omega-3 Fatty Acids." *HOPES.* Retrieved June 24, 2016. http://web.stanford.edu/group/hopes/cgi-bin/hopes_test/omega-3-fatty-acids/.

Luskin, Casey. "Following Appendectomy, a Higher Incidence of Cancer Suggests an Immune-Function of Appendix." *Evolution Views and News.*

Last modified July 2, 2015. www.evolutionnews.org/2015/07/people_who_unde097321.html.

McKay, Pat. "A Book Review of Pottenger's Guide to Cats—A Study in Nutrition." www.ectownusa.net/mineralcountynevada/docs/Potenger's%20 Cats%20book%20review.pdf.

Mercola, Joseph. "MSG: Is This Silent Killer Lurking in Your Kitchen Cabinets." Mercola.com. Last modified April 21, 2009. http://articles.mercola. com/sites/articles/archive/2009/04/21/msg-is-this-silent-killer-lurking-in-your-kitchen-cabinets.aspx.

———. "Sugar May Be Bad, But This Sweetener Called Fructose Is Far More Deadly." *Mercola.com.* Last modified January 2, 2010. http://articles.mercola. com/sites/articles/archive/2010/01/02/highfructose-corn-syrup-alters-human-metabolism.aspx.

———. "Sugar Substitutes—What's Safe and What's Not." *Mercola. com.* Last modified October 7, 2013. http://articles.mercola.com/sites/articles/ archive/2013/10/07/sugar-substitutes.aspx.

———. "Toxic Toothpaste Ingredients You Need to Avoid." Mercola.com. Last modified September 9, 2015. http://articles.mercola.com/sites/articles/ archive/2015/09/09/toxic-toothpaste-ingredients.aspx.

———. "Why Did the Russians Ban an Appliance Found in 90% of American Homes?" Mercola.com. Last modified May 18, 2010. http://articles. mercola.com/sites/articles/archive/2010/05/18/microwave-hazards.aspx.

Nachman, K. E., G. Raber, K. A. Francesconi, A. Navas-Acien, and D. C. Love. January 2012. "Arsenic Species in Poultry Feather Meal." *The Science*

*of the Total Environment.* Retrieved May 8, 2014. www.ncbi.nlm.nih.gov/
pubmed/22244353.


Netterstrøm, Bo, et al. 1999. "Relation Between Job Strain and Myocardial
Infarction: A Case-Control Study." *Occupational and Environmental Medicine*
339. Retrieved June 28, 2016.


Organic Consumers Association. "What's Wrong with Food Irradiation."
Organicconsumers.org. Last modified February 2001. www.organicconsumers.
org/old_articles/irrad/irradfact.php.


Palmer, Brian. "Cooking Up Cancer?" *Slate Magazine.* Retrieved June 24,
2016. www.slate.com/articles/health_and_science/medical_examiner/2014/01/
cancer_risk_from_grilled_meat_is_it_time_to_give_up_smoked_and_fried_
foods.html.


Rodu, B. 2011. "Carcinogens in Coffee and Smokeless Tobacco: Truths
& Half-Truths." Tobacco Truth. Retrieved November 13, 2014. http://
rodutobaccotruth.blogspot.com/2011/11/carcinogens-in-coffee-and-smokeless.
html.


Savory, Kristin. "Choosing Food-Based vs. Synthetic Supplements.
Empowered Sustenance (blog). http://empoweredsustenance.com/
food-based-synthetic-supplements/.


Schmidt, Charles W. 2013. "Arsenical Association: Inorganic Arsenic May
Accumulate in the Meat of Treated Chickens. [Published erratum appears in
*Environ Health Perspect* 2013 (Aug.), 121, no. 8 A241]. *Environmental Health
Perspectives* 121, no. 7: A226-A226 1p.  Retrieved June 16, 2016.

Schmidt, Michael. June 4, 2010. "A Tale of Two Calves—One Calf Was Fed on Raw Milk, the Other on Pasteurized." *The Bovine* (blog). https://thebovine.wordpress.com/2010/06/04/the-tale-of-two-calves-one-calf-got-raw-milk-the-other-pasteurized/#more-16769.

Silberstein, S. 2011. "Does Coffee Cause Cancer?" BeatCancer.org. Retrieved February 13, 2013. http://beatcancer.org/2011/01/does-coffee-cause-cancer/.

Solinas, M., S. Ferré, Z. You, M. Karcz-Kubicha, P. Popoli, and S. Goldberg. 2002. "Caffeine Induces Dopamine and Glutamate Release in the Shell of the Nucleus Accumbens." *The Journal of Neuroscience 22,* no. 15: 6321–24. www.jneurosci.org/content/22/15/6321.full.pdf/.

Squires, D., and C. Anderson. "U.S. Health Care from a Global Perspective: Spending, Use of Services, Prices, and Health in 13 Countries." *The Commonwealth Fund.* Last modified October 8,2015. www.commonwealthfund.org/publications/issue-briefs/2015/oct/us-health-care-from-a-global-perspective.

Studer-Rohr I., D. R. Dietrich, J. Schlatter, and C. Schlatter. 2016. "The Occurrence of Ochratoxin A in Coffee." *Food and Chemical Toxicology.* Retrieved May 28, 2015. www.ncbi.nlm.nih.gov/pubmed/7759018.

"Sweet, Sour, Salty, Bitter ... and Umami." Narrated by Robert Krulwich. Morning Edition. National Public Radio. November 5, 2007. www.npr.org/templates/story/story.php?storyId=15819485.

"The Importance of Omega-3 and Omega-6 Fatty Acids." *EUFIC* Last modified October 2008. www.eufic.org/article/en/artid/The-importance-of-omega-3-and-omega-6-fatty-acids/.

U.S. Department of Agriculture. "FSIS National Residue Program for Cattle."
Last modified March 25, 2010. www.usda.gov/oig/webdocs/24601-08-KC.pdf.

U.S. Food and Drug Administration. August 2002. "Guidance for
Industry: Action Levels for Poisonous or Deleterious Substances in
Human Food and Animal Feed." Retrieved February 8, 2016. www.fda.
gov/food/guidanceregulation/guidancedocumentsregulatoryinformation/
chemicalcontaminantsmetalsnaturaltoxinspesticides/ucm077969.htm.

Waters, A., T. Contente-Cuomo, J. Buchhagen, C. Liu, L. Watson et al. 2011.
"Multidrug-Resistant Staphylococcus Aureus in US Meat and Poultry." *Clinical
Infectious Diseases 52,* no. 10: 1227–30. http://dx.doi.org/10.1093/cid/cir181.

Westover, Arthur N., and Lauren B. Marangell. 2002. "A Cross-National
Relationship Between Sugar Consumption and Major Depression?" *Depression &
Anxiety (1091-4269)* 16, no. 3: 118–20. Retrieved June 17, 2016.

# Index